Family Business

Erin Potter-Plow

Dave Plow

For our boys.

Life asked death, "Why do people love me but hate you?"
Death responded, "Because you are a beautiful lie and I am a painful truth."

Author Unknown

CHAPTER ONE

The dirt is starting to get in my shoes. I've been standing in a fresh grave for the past forty-five minutes, digging out the sides to make sure it's the right shape for the coffin to be lowered in.

The sun beats down on me and sweat drips in my eyes. The smell of dirt is cool and dank in the afternoon heat. I'm almost done digging, and I know this because I'm six foot three and only have to dig six feet deep.

My dark curly hair is matted with damp soil and sweat, and all I can think about is how good a shower is going to feel once I get home. My eyes sting. I like digging graves. When the sun shifts toward the west it gets nice and shady.

Footsteps crunch toward me across the cemetery lawn.

"You almost done? I need you to be out of sight before the family gets here. You know the drill."

"Yeah Dad, I know. I'm pretty much done now."

"Pretty much done isn't done."

Dad is always wanting to hurry up and move on to the next thing. His goal in life is to make as much money as possible, and you can only do that by squeezing every moment of work out of every day.

He loves to stand over me. On level ground I'm taller than him, and he hates it. It's like by simply being born I became a direct threat to his status as head of the family and the family business. The sun glistens on his shiny bald head and drips of sweat threaten to stain the starched white collar of his dress shirt. The buttons on the navy blazer bulge, wanting desperately to pop off from the tremendous pressure of being forced closed over his round belly.

He's the funeral director. He runs the funeral home, oversees the cemetery, and is in charge of the body removal technicians. He's trained me my whole life to become a funeral director. Next in line for the crown. I'm happy to keep digging graves, but he's pushing for me to be a corpse dragger—that's what he likes to call the body removal guys.

He turns at the sound of an engine coming up the long drive of the cemetery. "Kyle's here. I gotta go."

I've known Kyle since I was a toddler. He's been my dad's right-hand man for years.

Dad offers me his hand and helps me up into land of the living again

"Dave, my man! Guess what tomorrow is?" Kyle says, looking at me

"What *is* tomorrow, Kyle?"

"Your first day on dragging duty."

I glance at my dad, who wears a proud grin spread across his red, overheated face.

"Seriously?"

"Yep. I'll pick you up at your place at 8 a.m. Be ready and waiting outside."

And with that, I'm suddenly promoted from cemetery caretaker to body removal technician. No one bothered to ask me if it was what I wanted, but I guess that's what happens when your dad is the one calling all the shots in your career.

The next morning I put on my white button up shirt and tie, my black slacks and loafers, and a dark blue blazer. It buttons easily, with no bulge. Looking at myself in the long mirror on the back of my bedroom door, I feel like a kid playing dress up. A five o'clock shadow is showing up already

2

even though I just finished shaving. I know my size makes people think I'm older—and tougher—than I really am. I don't mind if people think I'm intimidating. It makes life easier because they leave me alone, but nothing is further from the truth. I'm a fresh-faced optimist with a brand new driver's license and high hopes for success in the real world.

Like all fresh-faced optimists, I have absolutely no idea what I'm doing. I decide that the best way to approach this job is to simply act like my dad. Not scared, not nervous, not naive. I will project an air of professionalism and confidence.

I stand there looking in the mirror, trying to practice not smiling. Dad always says the worst thing a body removal technician can do—aside from dropping a body—is to appear happy.

"This is the worst day of these people's lives," Dad once told me. "You'll look like an insensitive asshole if you show up smiling."

I practice until I feel I have my expression just right. Not too relaxed, not sad, just neutral. Serious face only. I imagine I'm a guard at Buckingham Palace in one of those giant black hats, but that makes me laugh and ruins the neutral face I'm going for. I grab my pack of smokes and head outside to wait for Kyle to pick me up. I have no idea how today is going to go, but I'm as ready now as I'll ever be.

Kyle pulls up in a giant black Chevy Suburban and the morning sun reflects off the tinted windows. I climb in, sitting shotgun while Kyle drones on about what to expect from the job. He casually glazes over most of the actual details, not bothering to give me advice on how to deal with all the disgusting, fucked up things I know I'm going to see. He mostly focuses on things like traffic. I can expect to get stuck in traffic a lot, so it's okay to drive on the shoulder of the highway if I need to. Also, I can get free coffee at the funeral homes if I'm nice to the secretaries, and I can get extra gloves from the coroner's assistants since my dad is too cheap to order enough to keep in stock at the office.

My dad never talks about what it's like to see dead bodies all day long. Most of the men who do this job drink to cope. I'm not old enough to decide whether a life of heavy drinking is for me. Nineteen is still full of possibilities.

"So Kyle... When you see something horrible, how do you deal with it?"

"What do you mean?"

"I mean, you can't scream or puke or anything at the job site, so what do you do?"

"You have to turn all that shit off. No feelings, no reactions. Don't open that door to let your feelings out, or else you'll end up in the loony bin. Just pretend it doesn't bother you, and eventually it won't."

I'm not sure that's something I can do. I had a hamster once that I forgot to feed for a while, and when it died, I cried for days. Of course, I was five then. Maybe I'm better at coping now. Of course, there's a huge difference between a dead hamster and a dead human.

The shift is five days a week, on call twenty-four hours a day the whole time. I'm not sure how that's going to go. I enjoy my sleep. But if my dad could do it for the past twenty years, I can do it too. It probably just takes some getting used to.

Today we have one call. It's an airport run to pick up a body being shipped in from another city. Kyle pulls into a short-term parking space.

"Okay, so you'll go up to the ticket counter and tell them you're here for the HUMMER." He snorts with laughter. I don't get the joke.

"Why is it called a HUMMER?"

"Human. Remains. HUMMER." Kyle enunciates, like I'm a total idiot for not getting it.

"Shouldn't it be a HUM*REM*, then?"

Kyle's grin quickly turns to a frown. Clearly this is his favorite joke and he's irritated that I've robbed him of a laugh he feels is well deserved.

"I didn't name it, that just what we call it. We'll go in together, load the cardboard box with the body in it onto the stretcher, and take it to the funeral home. Easy stuff."

"The airline ships bodies in cardboard boxes? That's depressing."

"They try not to make it known there's a dead body on board. A basic cardboard box with no writing on it is as incognito as it gets."

I don't even get a glimpse of the body.

Afterward we head to a greasy spoon diner for lunch. This particular greasy spoon is called Lucille's Pie Hut and it's my favorite place in the world. My dad used to bring me and my brother there when we were kids.

Turns out it's been a hot spot for people in the funeral industry since it opened in the twenties. Coroners, funeral directors, corpse draggers, and cops all flock here for two reasons: one is it's open twenty-four hours, seven days a week. The other is for the pie. It's the best pie in the city, and the pastry chef invents a new one every week just to keep from getting bored. Today's pie is something called a "Bear Claw Bonanza", filled with chocolate chips, banana slices, and peanut butter chunks.

"So, what do you think so far?"

"It seems fine, like I remember growing up."

"Not the restaurant, dummy. The job."

"Oh. That's fine too. I mean, we really haven't done anything yet, have we?"

"Just you wait. Pretty soon you won't be able to get away from the job. It'll be everywhere you turn. You'll feel like you're going insane because you see death everywhere."

"Is that what you see every day?"

"Nah, not anymore. Like I said, you just flip the switch and turn that shit right off."

CHAPTER TWO

I spend my second day on the job at home playing video games in my pajamas, feeling pretty optimistic. I rent a room in an old house on the south side. I live with three roommates and four cats. Not my cats. I hate cats. The old craftsmanship is cozy. Ideal for me. Month to month, with everything included in the rent. Power, water, garbage. The only shitty thing is the house is right next to a giant catholic church. The bells ring at horrible times, but otherwise, the Catholics are perfectly amicable neighbors.

At 7:30 p.m. my phone rings. It's Dad.

"Kyle is on his way to get you. You two have a call."

I dress quickly and pull on my dress shoes, feeling well-rested and in a good mood. I'm excited to see what the night brings. I'm ready for something a little more exciting than a cardboard box pickup.

Kyle and I pull up in front of the apartment building and find two cops outside waiting for us. The building is old and creepy in the dark of the evening. It's probably a normal-looking building during the day. Right now, there's a single light bulb in the entryway, shining way too bright, like a maintenance man just stuck in a bulb he found laying around in the basement.

The building is painted a slate gray that reminds me of a hospital or jail. There are absolutely no sounds coming from inside the building. No TV blaring, no babies crying. Nothing.

As we walk up the steps, one of the cops tosses Kyle the keys.

"He's in number six on the first floor, in the bathroom."

"It must be a stinker," Kyle mutters as we wheel the gurney down the hall.

"What's a stinker?"

"You'll see. It's a corpse so rotten that people can't get far enough away from it to escape the smell. It usually happens when they've been dead for a while before they're found."

The closer we get, the stronger the smell is. I know that smell. I've been smelling it since I was a child riding with Dad while he took bodies to the morgue. I know it from the way my dad's clothes smelled. My mom would hang his work clothes in the basement, because there's no getting that smell out.

We silently walk down the first-floor hallway to the last door on the left and enter the unlocked apartment. We walk through the cluttered living room toward the bathroom. As soon as I see the dead man, the rest of the world disappears. I can't look away.

He's badly decomposed, a putrid green color from head to toe. What's left of his skin is covered in ruptured blisters where the blood has pooled. His head is swollen like he's had an allergic reaction to a bee sting. His eyes are swollen shut too. His cheeks and lips look like they might pop.

This is the moment of truth. Part of me wants to scream and run. To rip off my tie in a dramatic declaration and quit. I fight the urge to cover my eyes and run out of that nightmare bathroom. Another part of me, with my youthful hubris, wants to prove I have the guts to be part of this team.

Kyle watches me to see what I'm going to do.

Is this what death really looks like? How have I been so insulated from the disgusting reality my entire life? Does he not have any family? Why did no one find him sooner? Is that his tongue peeking out of the side of his cheek where the skin has split? Can a tongue be that color?

7

I close my eyes and try not to breathe too deeply. I need to suck it up and get this job done. And that's exactly what I do.

I bend down and prepare to grab the dead man with gloved hands.

"Wait. You can't just grab them, kid. The skin slides off like an over-boiled chicken."

For fuck sakes, this is getting worse by the second. I try not to shudder. I don't want Kyle to see any moment of weakness in me.

"Here, it's easy. Just set up the stretcher and slide him onto it—but first I'm going to teach you the towel trick," he says calmly, like a mentor demonstrating to his protégé how to perform a delicate task, as if we were repairing the cogs on a pocket watch.

Despite the gruesome scene in front of me, I manage to play it cool on the outside. I show no fear, no emotion of any kind. I tell myself this is not a rotting corpse. This is just a package I need to move from one place to another. My stomach lurches and I taste bile in my throat. I'm barely able to suppress my urge to scream.

We get him out the door and loaded into the Suburban without a word between us.

"You gonna make it, Dave?"

"I'm fine. Totally good. Totally cool, cool, cool..."

When we get to the morgue, he takes the stretcher in by himself. I sit in the car, trying to decide if I'm going to answer my phone the next time it rings. This is it. This is my chance to say fuck this job. This is the fork in the road, where I'll forever look back to and say, "yep, that's when I decided". Shit. First, I have to decide. Fuck. Fuck. Fuck. On the one hand, it's a job that's being handed to me that pays a shit ton of money. On the other, it's beyond fucking disgusting.

"I'm gonna drop you at home. That's enough for one night," Kyle says as he jumps into the driver's seat.

"Do you think that guy was in pain when he died?"

"That right there, you can't do that. That will make this job impossible. You can't think of them as people. I mean, they are, and you have to be respectful, but you don't need their names, their backstory, their details. All those things do is make it harder to do your job. Be like a surgeon that just swoops in, operates, and then gets out of there and lets someone else deal with the details. You can't get too involved or you'll drown in the horror."

I nod and we ride in silence the rest of the way to my house.

When I walk in the door, all three of my roommates are there. They're drinking beer and watching a boxing match on TV. It's weird. I dealt with a dead body and all they did was run to the store for beer. How can they sit there like that's normal?

"What was it like?"

"Was it horrible?"

"Was it a naked chick?"

"No, it was a guy. He was super…gross. Hand me a beer."

How could they possibly understand what it was really like? There are no words for the things now burned in my memory. I can't describe the smells or the sounds. They would have no point of reference. Maybe this is why my dad didn't have many friends outside the industry. Regular people wouldn't understand.

CHAPTER THREE

Frantic guitar and pulsing bass pour out the open front door of the bar. I finish my smoke, flick the butt into the street, and head inside.

I have a pocket full of cash and no plans tonight, so it didn't take much for Henry to convince me to come with him after our shift was over. I need a night away from the job. It's been a long five-day stretch.

"You're gonna love this band. They're a kickass punk rock band in town from L.A.," Henry says with a huge grin on his face.

After that first day with Kyle, I was paired with Henry for the rest of my training. We instantly clicked. Henry seems to know exactly when to make a joke to break the tension, and I love him for it. We can laugh at some of the worst things and commiserate over missing episodes of *Jerry Springer* because of the job. We've spent countless hours at Lucille's eating pie and bullshitting.

The bar walls are painted black and covered in old gig posters from shows long ago. There are two glaring fluorescent lights blasting the band in the face, but otherwise the only lights in the place hang over the two tables in the very back near the bathrooms. The whole building smells like stale beer, but that's a hell of a lot better than the smell I'm covered in all the time now.

"How have you never listened to punk rock?" Henry shouts over the music.

"I don't know, I've just always liked metal better. I guess I've never really given it a chance, because this is awesome!"

Since high school I've been a metal head, but as we stand in the bar, the short, catchy riffs of the grunge-punk band are infectious. I grab a beer and feel all the stress of the day melt away as the alcohol warms me.

Henry grabs my arm from behind. I didn't even realized I wandered closer to the stage. There are only about ten people at the front, probably because it's a Tuesday night.

"There's my buddy I was telling you about. Come meet him!"

I nod and follow Henry back to one of the rickety tables near the bathroom. The smell of stale beer is quickly replaced with the smell of urinal cakes and bleach.

I'm struck by how happy Henry looks outside of work. His mop of red curly hair seems more wild and free than it did this morning. He peeled off his white button up as soon as we clocked out, and under it he wore a sleeveless band T-shirt. The Accused. Must be another punk band. I have to Google them when I get home. Henry's arms are a pale blueish-white and covered with freckles. Little tufts of red hair stick out from under his arms. His chubby bearded face lights up as we got closer to his friend.

"This is the guy I was telling you about. Dave, this is Joel. Joel, this is my buddy from work, Dave."

I nod at him. It's impossible to have a conversation over the music.

"Joel has the best weed, and if you ever need mushrooms, he's your guy," Henry shouts.

Joel looks like a blonde version of Henry, but instead of a frizzy red beard, Joel is clean shaven and missing one of his front teeth. He grins like a goofy kid over Henry's endorsement. "Want to go smoke a joint in the alley?" He asks.

I nod in agreement and we head for the back door that leads onto a patio in the alley. It's a brisk night and the windy night air is a welcome break from the stuffy bar.

"So you're a corpse dragger too?" asks Joel.

"Yep."

"How is it so far?"

"Meh. It's fine. Better than flipping burgers."

"I think I would love that job. Can you put in a good word for me? I'm always asking Henry, but he says he doesn't have any pull there. But you're the boss' kid, right? You can get me in!" Joel grins his big goofy grin.

"Yeah, maybe. Can I buy a dime bag? I've been having trouble sleeping when I'm on call and I want to smoke myself into a coma."

"For sure!"

Joel hands a joint to Henry and we stand in a circle, smoking. This is the life. I have money in my pocket for a night out on the town, new friends, and good music. I'll hit the drive thru at McDonald's on my way home and this will officially be the best end to a long first week.

My phone buzzes in my front pocket. I already knew who it is.

"Hello?"

"Hey, can you get down to the waterfront? I need you to pick up a floater that just washed up," says my dad.

"I'm off shift and I'm busy." I do my best not to sound stoned.

"So what? Every body we pick up means more money in our pockets. Get your ass down there."

"No. I'm busy."

"Did you not hear me? I don't give a shit what you're doing. Making money is more important than trying to get laid, or whatever it is you're doing."

"Dad, I'm not going. I'm busy."

"You work for me, and when I tell you to get somewhere, you fucking get there. Now!" He hangs up.

"What should I do?" I ask Henry.

"Are you too stoned to drive?"

"No, not technically, but I sure as hell don't want to go see a body right now."

"You know your dad. He goes nuts when he thinks he's missing out on a buck."

"True. But if I go now, he'll think he can call me anytime and demand I jump when he says so."

"Yeah. But Dave, he already knows he can. That's why he did."

Shit, he's right. I'm dependable, and that means he can lean on me to do anything because he knows I will. Damn it. I hand the joint off to Joel. "Hey, thanks for the joint. I'll get your number from Henry and call you soon."

"Sounds good," says Joel as he takes a large hit from the joint.

I wave goodnight to Henry and head back to my van, hating myself for being so obedient. I should be enjoying my night off, not going on another call. But the money is so good, how could I not do it?

I can't show up to a scene stoned, so I stop at McDonald's first and have a bite to eat. I don't know why a Filet-O-Fish is so tasty when it's just a glorified fish stick on a gross sweet bun, but it is. A giant Coke and some fries round out my meal, and I feel like I'm sober again.

I pull up to the waterfront parking lot filled with first responder vehicles and hop out to light a smoke. I stay standing by my van because I want a chance to assess the scene. My dad is talking with the police. To his left is a stretcher with a body on it, I think. There's a small crowd of people gathered outside the police tape and a news crew setting up.

My dad spots me and waves me over. I hate the waterfront. It's all tourist restaurants and little shops that sell knickknacks. It doesn't feel like the rest of the city. It feels far too clean and perfect. I guess that's the point of a tourist district.

I toss my smoke on the ground and stub it out with the toe of my shoe. I take my time on purpose. I don't want to him to think I'm a trained dog. I close the gap between us and smell the sharp, fishy scent of ocean water. The city sits on an inlet that comes straight in from the Pacific Ocean, and there's no escaping the smell this close to the shore. I instantly regret my meal choice.

"Nice of you to finally join us."

"I'm here now. What do you want me to do?"

My dad looks me up and down, glaring like I've just insulted his tie. "You see that stretcher with a body bag on it? Go put it in your van and take it to the morgue. You know, do your job."

I can't help it. I roll my eyes at him.

"You got something to say to me?"

We stare each other down for what feels like an hour but probably lasts only ten seconds.

"Nope," I say as I turn and head for the stretcher.

I start to wheel it toward the van when the smell coming off it hits me square in the face. It's a stagnant rotten fish smell mixed with a putrid stink. I have to get this to the van quickly or I'm going to puke. I manage to make it halfway there before my stomach churns and there's no stopping it. I vomit violently onto the concrete, splattering my shoes with sick.

When the heaving stops and my stomach is empty, I hear it. Applause. My dad and all the first responders are gathered in a circle, laughing and pointing and clapping at me. I want to shrink inside my coat and disappear. Instead I wave and smile and wipe my mouth and try to pretend like I'm sharing in the joke instead of being the butt of it. My dad is such an asshole.

CHAPTER FOUR

It's 7:30 a.m. when the call comes in and I roll out of bed. I down two cups of coffee with lots of sugar and head out the door with a lit smoke in hand. I sit in my driveway letting my van warm up in the frigid winter temperature.

I pull into the train station and meet up with Henry. He's as bleary-eyed and frozen as I am and nestled inside an oversized, puffy orange snow coat that leaves his chubby face peeking out. He looks like a radioactive marshmallow. With a quick nod we set off to find the detective in charge. We wade through a sea of pant suits and briefcases, puffy coats and scarves, dirty looks and complaints to get to the scene. The El trains are always packed at this time of the morning: rush hour.

"I'm never going to make my morning meeting at this rate!" a woman shouts to no one in particular. She gnaws absent-mindedly on her perfectly manicured red nails. Her dark hair sits atop her shoulders in large curls that don't budge an inch despite the wind. She's pretty, but her face is all scrunched up in anger.

"Of all the days this could happen, why did it have to be today?" a man whines. He sucks on a cigarette and chugs his coffee, leaving his putrid, smoky breath hanging in the air as he complains.

Henry and I stand just outside the police tape, waiting to be told when we can pick up the body. Finally, a uniformed officer looks our way and waves at us to join him on the other side of the tape.

"What have we got?" I ask the officer. He shrugs and points to a man in a long coat holding a tiny pad of paper. Must be the man in charge.

"What have we got?" I ask again, though this time I ask the right person.

The detective, probably in his mid-fifties, glances up from his pad of paper. He looks me up and down and lets out a long, patronizing chuckle. His thin mustache looks glued to his upper lip and wiggles as he laughs. His skinny, pinched face is covered in deep wrinkles. Maybe he's spent far too many afternoons in the sun, squinting as it beats into his eyes, thinking about things that piss him off.

"What have we got? I'll tell you what we've got. We've got a guy splattered into a million pieces that all need picking up. This asshole jumped in front of a train that was going fifty miles an hour."

I know he thinks I'm a dipshit in way over my head, but it's fucked up to call the dead guy an asshole.

"Alright. Well, I guess we'll just get started, then."

"My hero," he snorts.

We have to walk down the tracks a couple hundred yards to retrieve the dead man. The tracks sit twenty feet above the ground, and I hate heights. There are chunks of meat everywhere. Red splatters cover the blanket of perfect white snow that coats the entire area.

Henry and I begin the painstaking process of finding the man and all his pieces. More snow comes down, quickly covering up what we're looking for.

The cops have already shut down the line we're working on, but the line headed in the opposite direction is still operating on time. Every eight and a half minutes we have to stop and brace ourselves while the train races by. Between the snow and the high perch I'm teetering on, I'm miserable.

Two cops try to help find the pieces ahead of us in the search party. Every so often one of them shouts *"arm!"* or *"leg!"* One of the cops stops abruptly. I catch up to him and notice the confusion on his face. He looks up at me and down again at the ball of flesh and meat and yellow fat on the ground in front of him. He struggles to find words for what he's thinking.

"I think this is one of the guy's eyes."

I look down and see a white orb that could be an eye, but there's no iris, no color, nothing. "There's no way that's an eyeball."

"That is one hundred percent an eyeball. I'm sure the color part just scraped off or something," the cop snaps at me.

"That's not really how eyes work. The color goes all the way through. This isn't an eye."

"Well, since you know so much about anatomy, what the fuck is it?"

Great. Another cop who thinks I'm just a jerk-off. All I want is the same respect I'm expected to give them. I don't get to tell a cop to fuck off. I'm not allowed to cuss at them or even give them dirty looks. But here this asshole thinks he can talk to me like I'm a goddamn garbage man picking up trash that a racoon strewed around his yard.

I take a deep breath and calm my temper a bit. "I don't know everything about the human body, but I know that's no eyeball."

I will be calm. I will be professional. I will not lower myself to his level.

"Whatever. Just put it in the bag and get it the fuck out of here with the rest of what's left of this cock-sucker. I can't believe someone would just jump like that. Now I'm stuck here in the snow freezing my bag off, picking up eyeballs."

Henry and I are the ones stuck picking up body parts. He just has to point at them.

Henry and I find all the parts—the most important ones, anyway—and get them off to the morgue where they belong. We drop the body bag on an exam table and head to the office in the back to wait for the coroner. Today,

James is on shift.

Henry and I watch from the office as James enters the exam room, unzips the bag, quickly looks over the body and parts, zips the bag back up and heads over to join us in the office.

"Hey! That cop who was helping us, he thinks the white ball is an eyeball. It's not, is it?"

The coroner chuckles. "No sir, that's no eye. Both eyes are still in the skull. That right there is probably a testicle, and I feel sorry for any man that can't tell an eyeball from a testicle."

James is the most fun of all the coroners. He knows everything there is to know about the human body. He knows of countless ways to die and all kinds of death-related trivia. The best thing about James is that he knows more about comic books than even I do, and that's saying something.

The morgue is weird. It always feels like it's nighttime because there aren't any windows, but that's because it's underground. The cheap fluorescent lights flicker in the halls just like in a bad horror movie. The smell of it stings my eyes and nose. All I smell is blood and disinfectant.

Coroner James and I debate whether there are any valuable assets Aquaman could bring to the Avengers. James' radically unpopular opinion is that there were a few, despite the Avengers being from the Marvel universe and Aquaman being from DC.

The office is the nicest part of the morgue. James has it decorated like the bedroom of a twelve-year-old. There are superhero posters on the wall next to one of Gillian Anderson from *The X-Files*. Someone has drawn a thought bubble above her gorgeous red head, reading "James is so much smarter than Mulder, and sexier too".

James sits, twirling his long handlebar mustache with one hand and picking the caramel corn he had for lunch from his teeth with his other hand. He always smells suspiciously like lilac, which is neither off-putting nor enjoyable. Just confusing. I've never known another man to choose lilac as their scent. He wears tiny spectacles at the end of his long upturned nose and keeps his graying hair dyed jet black and piled high on his head in a pompadour, with the confidence and air of a rooster. He's tall and slender, and always in a white lab coat, khaki shorts, and sandals with socks, even in the middle of winter.

Just as I launch into the most compelling part of my argument for why Aquaman would never survive ten minutes in a room with The Hulk, my phone rings and we head to the next scene.

"This isn't over. I will show you just how wrong you are about Aquaman."

"Maybe another day, sir. But that day is not today," James laughs.

CHAPTER FIVE

It's mid-morning and snow falls steadily, forming a heavy white blanket on everything. The wind whips violently as the sun hides behind the clouds, leaving a bleak gray day to contend with.

Henry and I climb into the van and make our way to the east side of the city, a notoriously run-down and crime-riddled part of town. There aren't many people out on the roads, probably because of the snow. We make our way to the apartment building and the dead man that's waiting for us there.

Henry's in the middle of showing me his very best Alice Cooper snarl from the passenger's seat when suddenly he yells at the top of his lungs. "*Look at that!*"

I scan the area and there, in all their glory, are two dogs fucking. We erupt into rolling laughter at the absurdity of two mutt dogs screwing in the middle of a snow flurry.

For a moment, all seems right and balanced in the world. While I escort the dead to their final resting place, life is still being created in the world, and soon there will be puppies, full of hope and innocence.

We arrive at the building. The Coronado. It's a notorious drug den for bachelors and college students. I maneuver around the emergency vehicles parked out front and take my parking spot among them.

The entry of The Coronado is lined with floor-to-ceiling mirrors, splattered with prominent gold veining that screams the seventies. The color scheme consists of faded avocado green for the carpet and a once-vibrant orange for the walls. Why does it smell like Aqua Velva aftershave in here?

We wheel the gurney down the hall of the first floor to the last apartment on the left. No one bothers us or stops us. We find an open door, and inside is Paige.

Fuck.

Paige is the new coroner. She's just transferred in from another city and is one of the most intriguing—not to mention irritating—people I have ever met.

She's only been with this coroner's office for a few weeks, but I've already heard from every guy I work with how much they want to fuck her. She's young and enthusiastic with long black hair she keeps swept off of her face in a loose braid that hits the middle of her slender back. She wears thick black-rimmed glasses and tons of makeup caked on way too thick. She wears bright red lipstick that she paints on just outside the line of her actual lips, making them look bigger than they are. And perfume. Did I mention the perfume?

"Well, Detective Rigby, I may look young, but I assure you I finished medical school. If you feel that way, Detective Rigby, you're welcome to call my supervisor."

She does this with everyone. Repeats their names over and over again in conversations with them. It's so annoying.

Crouching over the dead man—who doesn't look to be more than twenty—Paige talks mostly to herself now, but also for an audience of police officers. They just standing there, watching as the crime scene techs collect evidence and listening to Paige conclude how he died.

"He's in full rigor," she says. "He shows no outward signs of a violent attack. In fact, there is drug paraphernalia everywhere, yet no sign of an injection point to indicate an overdose. I guess we'll find cause of death in the autopsy."

"Have you checked in between his toes? Or..." Henry turns awkwardly to me and with a smirk. "His dick?"

Paige is just his type. He's been trying for the last few weeks to woo her into a date. No success, but kudos to him for his tenacity.

"Henry. What are you talking about, Henry?" She sounds annoyed.

I know what he's talking about, but I let him finish what he's started. I survey the room and it's entirely men, all except for Paige.

"Well, when guys are trying to hide their drug habits, they can't just shoot up in the normal places because they'll be covered in track marks. I bet you a coffee that guy has track marks all up and down the shaft of his dick. We see that a lot on the downtown east side. I guess you never got that in the small town you came from?"

"No, Henry. I can't say we ever did, Henry. Thank you so much for your suggestion."

I hope her constant name repeating is just a technique to learn people's names and not her regular speech pattern. Maybe it's a speech impediment, or a nervous tick. Maybe she has Tourette's and I'm being a total asshole. Either way, she's still extremely annoying.

The dead man is wearing one piece of clothing despite the snow outside: a pair of plaid, cotton boxer shorts. She pulls them off and pushes her glasses up her nose for an up-close inspection.

"Well I'll be damned if there aren't track marks, and even... Is that a point of infection that has started to fester? Here, look at it. Look closely!"

She tries in vain to get someone, anyone, to look at what she's excited to have found.

"We all got dicks here, lady. We know what they look like," the detective, Rigby I assume, snaps back at her.

She goes back to talking to herself while she fills out her paperwork, and before long we're given the all-clear to load the body onto the gurney.

Out we head, down the long hall to the snow-covered streets now being plowed. The city has managed to accumulate another few inches while we were inside. The snow comes down in sheets. Clearly this is going to be a storm we're just starting to see the nasty side of.

"Can you drop me at home after we get this guy to the hospital morgue?" Henry asks.

"Yeah man, of course. What have you got going on today?"

"I'm gonna relax properly. Smoke a joint, put on a record, and jerk off imagining Paige inspecting my dick like she just did for with dead guy's."

I feel a twinge of anger. Why? What do I care who jerks off thinking about her?

"Whatever you want. Just keep your phone on in case today ends up being busy."

I just want to go home, make a plate full of frozen burritos in the microwave, smoke a joint, and watch a marathon of old episodes of *Meerkat Manor*. I fucking love that show. Those little furry bastards are the cutest things I've ever seen. They help me forget about my day.

CHAPTER SIX

"You're going to the annual coroners dinner with me tonight, so go home and take a shower. Put on something nice. I want to introduce you to some important people."

I've just walked into the office, which is at the very back of the cemetery next to the parking garage and the crematorium, to drop off paperwork and get some more shrouds.

The shrouds are kept under lock and key. That's how cheap my dad is. They come in a Costco-sized box, but he only gives us each one or two at a time. I don't know how much they cost, but it definitely isn't so much that we couldn't each keep a box in our cars. The shrouds are just muslin cotton sheets we put over intact bodies while we transport them. Body bags are expensive and only used for messy pickups.

"Okay. Will there be decent food, or should I eat before we get there?"

"They always spring for steaks and salmon, so bring your appetite."

I've spent the day thinking I was going to be stuck eating whatever my vegan roommate made for dinner. Thursday is her night to cook for everyone, and we usually have a family-style meal together.

"Just don't drink the free booze. The coroners will always be shitfaced, but you can't be. Not when you're there representing me."

"You mean representing the company?"

"No. You're my kid. You represent me. Also, if you see Al Rosenthal there, don't get sucked into a conversation about his daughter. She's some spinster yenta he's trying to marry off to a nice Jewish boy with a successful family."

He slams the drawer on his file cabinet and heads out the front door. The office isn't really an office. It's an old construction site trailer that the foreman used to work out of, so when anyone slams anything, the whole trailer shakes. It still smells like machine oil and greasy sweat. The little AC unit in the window runs overtime in the summer trying to cool the 300 square feet, and the space heater in the corner does the same in the winter.

On the drive home, one thought keeps coming back to me: Paige is going to be there. She's so annoying. I wonder how much worse it is when she drinks. I'll have to make sure I steer clear of her. I wonder if she'll wear even more makeup than normal. Or more perfume, for that matter.

I rush in and shower. Our house may be aging, but the bathroom isn't, and it's by far my favorite place in the house. The tub shower is nice and big with plenty of head room for me, which is usually an issue. The tub was painted before we moved in, so it looks clean even if it's not. The fan is loud and covers any and all sounds that may give away what someone is doing. I love it. It makes up for the entire room being painted a powder pink. Even the ceiling.

I'm done and out the door in less than an hour. In the van, I roll down the windows. I don't want to get corpse stink back on me right away. Traffic is light and I make it there ten minutes early. My dad is already there.

We head inside the Four Seasons hotel together. The giant chandelier catches my eye first. I wonder if that's secure? I mean, I don't want it to fall and squish someone. Then I'd have to come pick them out of the pile of broken glass.

I try to shake the image, but it's has been happening to me a lot lately. I'm starting to see all the ways someone could die everywhere I go.

My dad struts down the corridor to the ballroom with confidence. I straighten up and lengthen my gait to match his. It really shows how much shorter he is than me when I walk tall.

He throws open the door to the Grand Ballroom and walks in like he owns the hotel. I let him get a few steps ahead of me. I hate watching him peacock like that when he's trying to impress people. It's embarrassing.

He immediately spots the person he wants to be seen talking to and heads their way, leaving me on my own in a huge room filled with people. Fancy tables covered in red tablecloths and ornate flower centerpieces are everywhere.

I don't see James or Paige or anyone else I recognize, so I head toward the bar. I want to grab a Coke and hope that I can blend in with the scenery. Hopefully no one will try to talk to me. I hate small talk with strangers almost as much as I hate these fancy-pants events.

I order the Coke and, with my back to the room, I hear it: Paige's shrill, ridiculous laugh. I turn and see her a few tables away. She must be wearing heels because she seems to tower over the woman she's talking to. She looks skinnier than usual, too. Her collar bone juts out from under the purple straps on her eggplant-colored dress. The dress goes all the way to her ankles. Her hair hangs in long, loose curls and her makeup is even thicker than usual. I begrudgingly admit only to myself that she's gorgeous.

Just then, she lets out another weird, snorting laugh. Now she looks more like a giraffe in a dress than a grown woman. I turn, but it's too late.

"Dave! I thought that was you! Come here!" She waves me over frantically.

"Hey, Paige. How's it going?"

"It's positively wonderful, David! I'm so glad you're here."

"Don't call me that. It's Dave. No one calls me David."

Her face scrunches up in a pout. "Okay, Dave. Dave, this is Sherry. She's the secretary for the medical examiner one county over. She loves horses and mac and cheese. Sherry, this is Dave, and...I don't think I know any interesting facts about Dave other than he doesn't go by David and he's a body removal tech."

I raise my glass and nod at the short, plump woman to whom Paige is gesturing. She looks as uncomfortable as I feel being reduced to a factoid introduction.

"Dave, come meet someone with me."

Paige grabs my arm and drags me off in the direction of the DJ booth, which I didn't even notice when I first walked in.

"You have to meet my friend Al. He is the nicest, most interesting person here tonight."

"Not Al Rosenthal, is it?"

"Yes! Do you already know him?"

I need a hard out, right now. Some luck I have that the two worst things that could possibly happen to me are currently happening. "No, but I need to go...see...if...wait, my phone's ringing. I gotta go." I wrench my arm free from her vice grip and head straight for my dad, at the same time putting my cell phone to my ear and pretending to answer a call. I feel her watching as I walk away. Maybe I hurt her feelings. Oh well. Better that than get roped into a blind date with a yenta spinster.

I walk up to my dad, putting my phone back in my pocket and sneaking a peek to see if she's still watching. She isn't. Someone else is in her sights and I'm free.

"Ah, good timing, Dave. Let's find our table and eat up. I'm starving." My dad takes off ahead of me again and I follow dutifully. I'm relieved to see our table is on the far side, away from Paige.

"You know you can't date someone from work, right?"

"What are you talking about, Dad?"

"That gigantic shiksa in purple with the clown makeup. You can't even

27

screw her. It's part of the contract I have with the coroner's service. No fraternizing."

"Don't worry. That is the single most annoying woman I have ever met in my life. I wouldn't touch her."

"Good, don't. Take it from me."

"What does that even mean?"

"Don't worry about it."

We sit through two keynote speakers before dinner is served. I'm so hungry, I'm actually eating the rock-hard bread rolls that have been on the tables for hours. The awards ceremony starts when dinner is served, and then finally, with dessert, is the guest speaker.

I start to daydream before the introduction of the guest speaker. Dessert tonight is tapioca pudding. Who serves tapioca pudding at a fancy dinner? Isn't that what they reserve for old people and kids? I imagine that something must have gone wrong in the kitchen.

"Where are all the tiny blackberry tartlets that I had planned for dessert?" the head chef would shout at the kitchen staff.

"Burned every single one of them, Chef. What are we going to do?" the sous-chef would say mournfully.

"I have just the solution!" the head chef would shout, "It's a classic dessert, the consistency of snot, with little lumps of booger-shaped mystery balls and one distinctly flat vanilla flavor. It's perfect!"

I chuckle to myself for a moment, lamenting how clever I am, when I realize my dad has been talking to me for the past few minutes and is waiting for me to respond. And he's not the only one. Everyone in the room is looking in my direction, waiting for me to answer a question that I didn't bother to listen to.

"Uh… What was the question?"

My dad's face breaks into an angry, bright red flush. He's boring a hole in my skull, waiting to see if I'll catch on and figure it out without any words actually passing between us.

"I said, aren't you going to introduce me? I'm the goddamn guest speaker tonight. That's why I gave you those notecards," my dad spits out through gritted teeth.

"I don't know what you're talking about. You didn't give me any notecards," I whisper back.

"Yes, I did. I gave them to you yesterday during lunch in the office."

"I didn't work yesterday, and I wasn't at lunch with you in the office."

His eyes widen with realization. "Get up there and say something nice about me or I'll kill you," he whispers.

I stand and head for the stage through the maze of fancy tables. I head up the stairs to the podium. "Ladies and gentlemen… It's my pleasure to introduce to you tonight, your guest speaker." I can't think of anything witty to say or even remotely flattering. My dad drags a finger across his throat at me from the table, so I simply say his name and start a spirited round of applause. He heads for the stage, all smiles. He climbs the stairs and hip checks me at the podium. I stumble a bit and catch myself before turning and heading off the stage as fast as my feel will take me.

Fuck. Tonight will forever be the night I fucked up his intro, not the night he forgot to give me the notes. I'm never going to hear the end of this.

CHAPTER SEVEN

I hate picking up hoarders. Mostly because it's such a pain in the ass to get the stretcher in and out, and this time is no exception. The building isn't that old, but the state of disrepair gives it the creepy feeling of a much older building. Light bulbs flicker in the halls and scratching noises echo from somewhere inside the walls. We head down the hallway to the apartment of the dead man.

I'm working with my dad today. Dad's always been a funeral director, but back when I was little, he used to work all aspects of the job, including body removal. I used to sit in the passenger's seat of the van and color or snack on my Happy Meal, waiting for him to finish so we could go back to whatever we were doing that day. I got so used to being around dead bodies all the time, it never seemed weird.

The paint on the front door is peeling and the top hinge is missing. When Dad and I reach it, the smell hits us. The place has all the usual stuff: giant towering stacks of old newspapers, a non-functioning toilet coated with black film, and hundreds of dolls. Creepy dolls. Sad, dirty dolls missing parts. Their creepy faces peer out from under mountains of garbage. It sends a shiver down my back because it's just so damn creepy.

Not every hoarder has bags of their own shit and piss laying around, but this guy does. It's so disgusting, you can't even smell the corpse over the smell of shit and mold, and who knows what the fuck else has combined in the putrid perfume.

The old man had carved out a little nest in the side of a small mountain hoard. A heaping mound of various sundries and spoiled snacks topped with old blankets and rotting clothes. Its peak reaches the ceiling.

He's sitting in a dirty old recliner chair. When we lift him, we see he's upgraded the chair by adding a hole in the seat with a toilet bucket underneath. The bucket is lined with an old grocery bag.

He died perched in his toilet recliner in front of the TV, which is only half visible because of a stack of empty Pop Tart boxes. Strawberry, the grossest of all the Pop Tart flavors.

Pieces of his face are missing. His rat roommates, as they are known to do, helped themselves to a buffet of his nose and most of his bottom lip after he expired. The man's nose-less face looks...peaceful. Maybe even happy. And just as horrible as one of his fucked-up dolls.

Standing there on a heap of old, used shit bags, two rats climb out of the pile next to the dead man and start fucking on an old pizza box. Ridiculous. Rats have no respect.

We get him outside, and just I slam the doors shut on the van my dad's phone rings.

"Get in, we've got another one. Guy stepped out in front of a bus," he says.

I'm not enjoying working with my dad. We never make small talk in the van, he just makes phone calls. I wonder if he makes small talk with any of the other guys.

We get to the intersection of Main and Cardinal ten minutes later to find a dead man dressed in nothing but an army fatigue jacket, a pair of boxer shorts, and flip flops. There's a city bus loaded with passengers with a giant dent in the shattered windshield where the dead man's head hit when he stepped off the curb.

The guy's mostly in one piece, with the exception of his right arm. I

31

start looking up and down the emptied street when my dad's phone rings again. Another call, and we don't even have all of this guy loaded up yet. Today is shaping up to be a bad one.

"What are you looking for?" Dad shouts from half a block away.

"His right arm. It's missing."

"This guy is clearly a veteran. He probably lost it in the war. Let's just load him up and go. The calls are starting to come in one on top of the other. It's a full moon, remember?"

"How do you know he was already missing an arm?"

"Why else would he kill himself? If I lost my arm in the war, I would do the same thing. Load him up, and let's go!"

I shrug. At this point, I've done a pretty thorough search of the area. I don't see an arm, so we load him up and off we go.

Halfway there, Dad's phone rings again. I'm so sick of hearing his annoying ring tone. It's the theme song from *The Odd Couple*. Low and behold, it's a cop at the scene we're speeding away from. The arm's been found. It had been ripped off and tossed ten feet in the air, landing on the outdoor patio of a first-floor apartment.

"Shit, we have to turn around and get his arm."

"Oh, you mean the arm he lost in the war?"

"Just grab the fucking arm and let's go. Every call means money, and the longer you take, the less money I make."

"Well, maybe next time we should take an extra five minutes to look around for missing limbs before we just take off to the next scene."

"Maybe. And maybe next time you think of something shitty you want to say to me, you can just remember that one of us built this business from the ground up, and the other one came out of my balls."

We ride in silence to the next call, putting off dropping the two guys at the morgue. Sometimes they stack up in the back.

After what seems like an eternity, we finish with the pickup at the retirement home and drop everyone off at the morgue. Without a word, my dad drops me at home and speeds off into the night.

I never drink when I'm on call, but after today, I need a drink, or a joint, or something. It's almost Christmas, and all I can find in the house is a bottle of cooking sherry and some peppermint schnapps. Figuring the schnapps is the better of the two, I drink and watched an *All In The Family* marathon. Still, the flashes of death and gore come. For every one that comes tumbling out of my brain and flashes across my thoughts, I take a drink. It only takes forty-five minutes to polish off the bottle.

I wake up to the phone ringing five hours later. The blinding light of mid-morning blasts me as soon as I open my eyes. I answer it knowing full well what I'm going to hear.

"Hope you got some rest. Get up and get ready."

"Fine. Text me the address and I'll meet you there."

I hang up without letting my dad respond. While making my way to the bathroom, the wave of drunkenness hits me in the face. I want to vomit and crawl into a dark hole—preferably one that does not smell like Christmas—and sleep for two more days. I don't have the luxury of either option. My mouth tastes like a Christmas elf's asshole so I brush all the taste out as best I can and hit the road. Halfway to the call I pull over and throw up.

Best case scenario, this is going to be nice and easy. A quick set of paperwork filled out, a hoist onto the gurney, and away we go to the morgue. I need something greasy to soak up all the sick sloshing around in my gut, and McDonald's is the perfect place.

My favorite thing to do is drive up and order with a body in the back. When I get to the first window to pay, the person working the window is hit with the horrific stench of death. Mostly they look at me, their face scrunched up and wondering if I'm the filthiest person in the world. Can't I smell what's wafting out of my vehicle?

I pull up to the scene. It's an old heritage building that doesn't have loading zones out front. That means it's probably doesn't have elevators either because it's so fucking old. I grumble and double park, put the coroner's sign in the window, and turn on the hazard lights. Good enough.

As I pull out the stretcher, all I can think about is how much I want a McGriddle. I push the stretcher around to the sidewalk at the front of the building and trip on a small break in the concrete.

"Fuck!"

Dad and I climb the four flights of stairs to the apartment only to find a pair of firefighters hacking away at the door frame in an attempt to widen it. Not a good sign. Sure enough, a man has died in his bed. He's easily 600 pounds, and it's no easy task getting him onto the stretcher and then down four flights of stairs. More than once I stop and dry heave for a minute before I can continue. Thank god the two firefighters are watching and hop in to help us carry him down.

The four of us finally get him through the lobby and out the front door. We head to my vehicle, and inside I'm doing a little victory chant because I'm so close to my McGriddle I can almost taste it.

That's when it happens.

Heading backward up the sidewalk, the heel of my shoe catches on the very same split in the concrete as it did on the way in. This time when I trip, I don't just stumble momentarily and right myself. My ankle twists dramatically, and as I start to fall, I cry out, "*Fuck!*" Ever so elegantly and as manly as I can, I grab the corpse's legs to keep myself from tumbling backward. I hear a loud *pop, pop*, and with complete confusion I fall ass-first into a snow drift, two prosthetic legs clenched tightly in my hands.

"You just pulled his fucking legs off!" Dad yells.

"They felt like normal legs when we put him on the stretcher!"

We know that they're prosthetic legs, but many of the gawkers gathered outside the building do not. A girl wails dramatically "Oh my *gawd!*" as if the man's been dead so long that his limbs simply popped off with the least amount of pull.

My pants are wet, my ass is cold, my stomach's churning, and my ankle's killing me. I'm getting two goddamn McGriddles and some fucking coffee after all this bullshit.

CHAPTER EIGHT

"Dude, I can't believe you scored me an interview for this job, finally!"

We walk into the office trailer at the back of the cemetery for Joel's job interview. He whistles "Walking on Sunshine" while we make our way up the ramp to the front door. All I can do is shake my head. I have no idea how this is going to go. Is he really that excited for this job interview?

In the office, my dad sits at his desk reading invoices. He doesn't acknowledge that we're there. We sit in silence for a few moments.

"Good morning, sir. My name is Joel Richardson, and I'm so glad you decided to give me a chance to interview for the body removal technician job."

My dad looks blankly at Joel. He looks him up and down, trying to figure out if this is a joke. Joel's gotten a haircut for this. His blonde hair is gelled to the side of his face in a severe part on the side of his head, while in the back his mullet cascades down just past his shoulders. The mullet is for his on-stage persona, but that's totally lost on anyone who doesn't know him. He's wearing a faded blue button up shirt, now a steely gray. Below it are black slacks and bright-yellow Converse All Star tennis shoes.

Joel stands with his hand thrust forward, waiting for my dad to shake it. He doesn't. Classic Dad power move.

"Okay, Billy Ray Cyrus, can you be available to be on call twenty-four hours a day during your work week?"

"Oh, for sure!" He smiles.

"Are you bothered by the idea of dead bodies? Touching them, seeing them?"

"Not at all. My grandpa died in his chair at home and my grandma was so upset she just sat in his lap crying and wouldn't let anyone take him for almost six hours."

Another blank stare from my dad. "Do you have a driver's license?"

"Yes sir, I sure do. Got a seventy-six on my driver's test just last week." He flashes another big, goofy smile.

"Okay. We'll try you for a week and see how you do. Dave here can train you. Report back here Wednesday to fill out your paperwork."

"Thank you so much, sir. You won't regret this, I promise!" Joel turns on his heel and almost skips out of the office. The door slams behind him and I hear a long sigh from Dad.

"Is he retarded?"

I burst out laughing. Joel is goofy, but you can tell he's a fully functioning adult.

"No, seriously. I think that guy's retarded and he's trying to hide it."

"He's not retarded, he's just excited!"

"Does he know what we do here?"

"Yeah, of course he does."

"Mark my words, one day we're gonna find out that that guy's a frittata."

I clutch my abdomen and my eyes fill with tears from laughing.

"Oh, and just a heads up, I got a call yesterday from a guy I know over at the old folks home on the south side. They had a guy die with no family or next of kin, so I told him I would hold the body for him as a favor until arrangements can be made."

"Wait, hold him where? We don't have a cooler here."

"No, *we* don't." He's getting annoyed with me now. "But the hospital out by the high school for the deaf does and the guy there owes *me* a favor. Take the body over there next time you get a call out that way, would ya?"

"Where is he now?"

"He's here, behind the office in the underground parking area. It's cool in there. He'll be fine for a few hours."

"Dad, are you serious? You can't just leave a body outside!"

"Don't do that. Why are you always doing that? You challenge my authority on everything. Ever since you learned how to talk all you've done is challenge me! Now get out of my sight and take that body with you!" He stomps over to his desk and starts slamming things down. I stay put, waiting to see if maybe I can say something to convince him this whole thing is a bad idea. The phone rings, and as he grabs the receiver to answer he looks me dead in the eyes and gives me the finger.

Fuck it. I walk out. Whatever happens, it's on him.

"Oh man, I can't believe I nailed that interview!" Joel says. He's standing by the passenger's side door of my work van with an air of satisfaction.

"Just be careful with my dad. He's an asshole."

"He seems fine. A straight shooter, maybe, but that's okay with me."

"I mean it, Joel. He seems reasonable at first, but all it takes is one mistake to find yourself in the doghouse with him. And there's no getting out once you're in there."

"I think it's different with you because he's *your* dad. He's just going to be my boss."

"Okay, well, don't say I didn't warn you."

"Let's go celebrate! I've got a joint, money for a couple slices of pizza, and there's a free punk show at The White Owl that starts in two hours. What do you say?"

I look back at the office trailer. I can hear my dad yelling at whoever's on the other side of that phone call. I know I'm on call today, but I don't want to be anywhere near that man or this place right now.

"Fuck it. Let's do it. If my phone rings I'll deal with it, but for now let's go celebrate."

We share the joint in the van on the way to the pizza shop and talk punk rock. It's still nagging at me, what Joel said. Is he just an asshole to me because he's my dad? Isn't it supposed to be the other way around? Isn't he supposed to help me more because I'm his son? I'm growing to really hate working for family. It's so much more complicated than it feels like it should be.

"Look out!"

Without thinking, I slam on my brakes and come skidding to a stop on the side of the road. I'm so stoned it feels like it all happens in slow motion. "What? What is it? Was there a kid or something?"

"Nah man, a squirrel ran out in front of you. I didn't want to see you hit him."

I slap my hand to my forehead, filled with frustration and adrenaline.

"You can't do that for a squirrel, man. That was crazy!"

"I can and I will. You can't just run them over."

"I don't think you're going to last in this job, Joel, if you can't handle a squirrel being hit by a car."

CHAPTER NINE

"We should totally do it! It would be awesome!" Joel says, inhaling a giant hit off the joint we're sharing on the back porch of his house.

"I don't play an instrument, though. I mean, I sort of play drums, but like, not good or anything."

"Doesn't matter. Punk isn't about being good, it's about playing fast and fucking shit up!" Joel smiles at me.

"Fuck it, I'm in. Let's form a band and fuck some shit up!"

"Yes! Alright, first things first. What should our name be? We need a fucking badass name like Fetus Drip, or maybe Anarchy Plague." Joel's eyes widen with excitement.

"Let's not take ourselves so seriously. What if we did a funny punk thing? Like gross and over the top and funny and fast and—"

"*Fuck* yeah! That's it. That's our thing. We'll be gnarly, funny, punk rock!"

Our first band practice starts twenty minutes later. Joel frantically strums chords on his acoustic guitar like a maniac, flipping his mullet backwards and forwards while scream-singing gibberish. I've smoked so much weed that all I can do is focus on the beat. One, two, three, four, one, two, three, four, one, two, three, four…

It's overwhelming, just knowing that I can focus all my energy, all my rage, all my…*everything* on these drums. No dead bodies, no annoying shiksa giraffes, no Dad bitching at me to move my ass faster to pick up more bodies. It's just me and the beat. Just the music. I love this. I was born to do this. I want nachos.

Joel and I start going to every single punk rock show we can find in the lower mainland. It's infectious, the surging energy of the crowd all moving together in the chaos of the moment. Sweat and screams and shoving and slamming into each other. This is where I'm free. This is where I'm so much more than just Dave, the guy that picks up dead people. I'm just another punk rock guy lost in the music.

I walk up to each and every merch table at every show and buy everything I can get my hands on. What's the point of making good money if I can't spend it on whatever I want? I talk to the bands and find out where they're from. How long is their tour? Do they have records or just CD's? I want to know everything about how to do this.

"How are we gonna be able to tour if we can't both take time off work at the same time?" Joel asks me after a punk show one night over omelets and pie from Lucille's.

"I don't know. We'll figure it out. We have to tour, though. That's how you get your name out there and get famous and do it for a living. That's what Gene says. He's Shelly's roommate. He's a drummer."

"It would be sweet to see our name up on a marquee somewhere. 'The Hairy Areolas live at the Nike Arena'," Joel laughs.

"I'm telling you dude, first we play a show, then we go on tour. We get the fuck out of here and away from all the fucking death."

"I'm not going anywhere yet. I just landed this dream job!" Joel protests.

"Let's see if you still feel that way in a month or two."

"Maybe there's a way to do both. Either way, we can't do anything until we record some songs. We need a demo. That's the best way to start. Then we can send our shit to record labels and venues and bookers."

"Good point," I say.

"Hey, your dad was telling me the other day about how he once met Mel Brooks. How come you never told me that story?"

"What are you talking about? My dad has never met Mel Brooks," I say between bites of Marshmallow Manor Pie. It's a sickeningly sweet combo of marshmallow cream, butterscotch chips, and a graham cracker crust. It's absolute perfection.

"Yeah, he did. He met him at a funeral for one of Mel's uncles back in the seventies."

"How could that have possibly happened and he never told his own son?"

"I don't know, but it was so cool. Your dad saw him at the graveside and recognized him. I guess your dad dug the grave earlier in the day and he was waiting for the family to leave so he could come in and finish filling it in. Anyway, I guess your dad quoted some line from *Blazing Saddles* and they shared a laugh. It's a great story. You should ask him to tell it to you!"

"I didn't even know my dad has seen *Blazing Saddles*..." I feel like an asshole. One who isn't even worthy of a shitty celebrity-sighting story from my own dad. There's no way I'm going to ask him to tell it to me. That's exactly what he would love for me to do, beg him for crumbs when he's handing out sandwiches to a stranger he's called retarded more times than I can count.

"Uh... Have you come up with some new beats? I wrote a song last night about that feeling you get after you eat an entire large pizza in one sitting and then get diarrhea and hate yourself. I think you'll like it."

I let Joel change the subject because it's easier than admitting out loud that I have no idea how much my dad has compartmentalized his life, or all the things he hasn't included me in. Has he told my older brother that story? Does my mom know it? She would have been married to him at the time.

"That sounds amazing, man. What did you name it?"

"'Pizza Regret.'"

"Fuck yeah."

We sit in silence and finish our food. I can tell Joel feels sorry for me and I hate it so goddamn much I want to scream. He's looking at me like I need a hug. Damn it, he's going to try and hug me when we get up.

We stand up to pay the bill. He stretches his arms out and beckons me in, nodding as if it's okay for me to need a hug after such a tough revelation.

"Are you having a stroke? Put your arms down."

"Come on, Dave. I'm here for you, man. Dads are tough. The whole relationship thing is hard to balance and gets worse when you grow up."

"If you come at me for a hug, I'm gonna bash you in the balls."

"Okay. Well, if you ever need one, I'm here for you."

"Shit in one hand and wait for me to ask for a hug in the other and see which one fills up first."

CHAPTER TEN

Holidays are weird for death, but nothing comes close to Christmas for suicides. The first call of the day comes in Christmas morning. I'm still bright-eyed and bushy-tailed from having two days off. Henry and I walk in the front door of a trailer and find the dead man on the couch with a bullet hole in his head. On the coffee table in front of him are several boxes. Each gift has been carefully opened. None of the paper is ripped and none of the ribbons have been pulled off. It looks like he meticulously unboxed each gift and then shot himself.

"I guess he didn't like his presents," Henry says to no one in particular.

The morning quickly becomes a blur of coffee and long drives from one side of the city to the other, and then to the outskirts of town. Once you get a few miles from the center of the city there are rural farmlands that encircle it on all sides. A reminder that not so long ago this area was not a metropolis.

Another suicide. This one is an older woman who lives with her husband on one of the farms that remain standing. She left a note—and a long one from the looks of it—on the side table next to her chair in the living room. I know all I need to know. Her body needs to go to the morgue at Peace Valley General Hospital.

Henry and I load her into the van. As we stand smoking and chatting, his phone rings. We're the only two working today on account of me being Jewish and Henry liking the overtime. Later I'll have some Chinese food and watch *Die Hard,* as is my Christmas tradition.

"I need to grab my work van and head out to a call downtown. You need to take this one to the hospital to have a doctor pronounce her. All the coroners are tied up with other scenes. Drop me on the way, okay?" Henry says while jamming his phone back into his pocket and heading for the passenger's seat.

"I hate having a doctor call time of death. It takes forever to get anyone to stop what they're doing in the ER and come out to the van. All so I can drive around to the back of the building and load them into the morgue. Why can't they just meet me in the morgue? Then I can at least hang out in the coroner's office while I wait."

"Because all doctors are assholes," Henry states matter-of-factly.

He's right. One night I ended up waiting almost three hours for a doctor to come put their stethoscope on a corpse, say a time of death for my paperwork, and then fuck off. Total time spent with me: less than thirty seconds.

It seems like an annoying waste of time, but then again, it's proving to be a hectic morning. Maybe a break is a good thing. I drop Henry off and head to the hospital.

As soon as I walk in the doors of the emergency room, I see Kellie. Kellie is the nurse who seems to always be working when I come in. All her scrubs are purple and they're always covered in Garfield or some other cat. But never Nermal, to my disappointment. Garfield's annoying cousin is my personal favorite character.

Kellie has carrot-orange hair that she wears in a tight bun on the back of her head. Always. Light brown freckles adorn her high cheekbones and the end of her nose, and she never wears makeup. I like her, but I can't quite put my finger on why. She reminds me of Pippi Longstocking, the eccentric red-headed girl from the kids' books. She had a pet monkey and an absentee father who always left her behind while he had adventures on the high seas. Pippi, not Kellie.

"Hey, Dave! What are you doing here?" she chirps in a high-pitched, happy voice.

"I need someone to call time of death for the one I've got in the van. How busy is it today?"

"Oh, you know, the usual holiday crowds. Mostly burns from grease fires and overdoses."

"I'll just wait in the van, if that's cool. I'm parked out in the ambulance area."

"Sure. I'll send someone out ASAP."

Maybe I should ask her out sometime. I can see her being kind of fun to hang with, but it might get weird coming to the hospital if we ever broke up. Not worth it. Keeping it casual seems easier.

I want to sit in the van in peace and read the new book I got from Joel for Christmas. A history of Egyptian tombs. I don't really care about Egyptology, but I figure that would be more fun than sitting in a hospital waiting room with people coughing all over me. To my surprise, it only takes forty-five minutes for a doctor to come out. I've barely scratched the surface on the tombs of the pharaohs when the back doors fly open.

"Hey, you need me to pronounce, right?" the young female doctor asks me.

I twist around in my driver's seat to face her. "Yeah, if you could, that would be great."

"Sure. Time of death…11:27 a.m. Have a merry Christmas!" And with that, she slams the doors.

I shift into drive and check behind me to see an ambulance racing in. I figure I better get moving so I jam on the gas and swerve out of the space I'm parked in and onto the main road that leads to the back of the hospital.

Instantly I notice something is wrong.

When you close the back doors, you have to lift the latch on the left side door so that it locks into place, then close the door on the right. The doors swing wildly as I pull out onto the main road, and before there's time for me to process what's happening, the stretcher, with its wheels up and locked in, starts to slide out of the now-open back doors of the van. With the wheels up, it's a straight drop onto the black pavement. Sparks fly from the metal stretcher, grinding loudly as it hangs halfway out of the van. Good thing it's the bottom half, with the dead woman's feet.

I swerve onto the makeshift shoulder of the steep road, which is all gravel, and hop out. The stretcher has managed to get stuck on the trailer hitch, keeping it from falling all the way out. I quickly slam the doors shut and latch them before heading for the morgue.

After all the excitement of the morning I manage to have a few hours of down time. It's just past lunch time so I head for my favorite Chinese restaurant where the egg rolls are greasy and the coffee is strong. I sit alone in the quiet restaurant listening to Christmas songs that echo into the dining area from the kitchen.

Christmas songs always bothered me as a kid. They seemed like a constant reminder of what I was excluded from: the joys of Santa, a Christmas tree, gifts, and cookies. Not that we didn't have those things for Hanukkah, but it just wasn't the same. I never had anyone to hang out with on Christmas. They were always doing Christmas things, and that left me, the lonely Jewish kid, wishing that there was something on TV other than *Miracle on 34th Street.*

As I got older, it bothered me less. I didn't mind being left out of Christmas because it no longer meant being the only one to not get presents. It meant I was the only one not obligated to have awkward Christmas meals with relatives. No midnight mass or carols, no Christmas karaoke. I was fine with not being subjected to those things.

Just as the first few notes of "Santa Baby" begin to ring out across the empty, dingy room, my phone chimes. It's a text with an address on the other side of the city and the word "solo", meaning Henry's still busy with whatever call he's gone on.

I arrive to find two firetrucks and an ambulance. As is usually the case when I get called in, the EMTs are sitting in the truck, desperately trying to keep warm on the frigid winter day. As I pull out the gurney, I hear the firefighters loading their gear back onto the truck.

"What happened?"

"Gas. She put her head in the oven," says a young firefighter.

"Seems a bit dramatic."

I thought he might chuckle, but instead he gives me angry silence. Maybe he has yet to develop that morbid sense of humor that has been such a saving grace for me in this job.

Inside I see why my joke is not funny at all. The girl who put her head in the oven could not be more than fifteen years old. Her face is blue and her eyes are open in a permanent stare into nothing.

"Shit."

"Yeah. Fucking Christmas," says Paige.

I didn't even see her on my way in, and I jump—just a bit, but not enough for her to notice. I hope. She stands in the corner of the kitchen with her purple clipboard in hand, scribbling on paperwork. She looks like a candy cane elf today. Her long dark hair is split up the back of her head and carefully and intricately braided down either side. Her lips are a bright candy apple red, and while on any other day it would be a stark contrast with her pale skin, today she wears a red and white striped turtleneck and a pair of black slacks that cinch tightly just above her hips. She looks exactly like a grown-up elf. But much prettier.

In the harsh kitchen light I see the lines starting to form at the corners of her eyes and around the edges of her mouth. I guess the sleepless nights and long hours are getting to her as much as they're getting to me. I try to think of something else, but there's nothing to say. Why can't I think of anything to say?

We somberly finish our paperwork and go our separate ways. The firefighters head back to the station house. Paige heads for the morgue, and I'm sent out on what ends up being my last call of Christmas.

CHAPTER ELEVEN

While the van is warming up, I switch the dial on the radio, trying to find something to lift the fog of somberness that's overcome me. Back and forth I click the small knob, finally landing on a station that's playing my most hated song of the season: "White Christmas". I don't even know why I hate it. There's nothing offensive or even annoying about the melody or lyrics. It just rubs me the wrong way.

I pause, thinking how much I loathe the song, when out of the corner of my eye I notice a sign on the lawn of the home next door to the one I've just been in. In large, black letters on a sign that's as big as the windshield of the van, someone has painstakingly written, "No Jesus, No Peace. Know Jesus, Know Peace". It snaps me out of the funk that's settled in and I chuckle to myself. I don't even know why. Maybe it's the simplistic hopefulness of the sentiment, or maybe it's just because of what I picture when I think about it. I picture a sassy gay man lecturing a room full of dead people waiting to get through the pearly gates, waggling his finger and wiggling his hips back and forth, reciting the verse.

Goddamnit, I'm getting tired. How can I be this tired already?

My phone chimes again. Text from Dad. It's an address for me, so off I go. I'll get the second body before heading to the morgue. In the thirty-degree chill there's no need to worry about smell or decomp. No rush.

I pull up to the empty corner lot in old downtown. Henry's already there. His face is pinched as the winter winds whip at us in the early evening dusk.

"What did you end up having to do?"

"Suicide, of course," Henry chuckles. "Guy hung himself from the steel bridge downtown. It took forever for the coast guard to get him down. I froze my balls off! All I can think about is how much I want a giant bowl of ramen noodles, a beer, and a good movie."

Henry and I stand on the sidelines, waiting to be told to move in. Henry has his own van and we decide to load this one into his. That way we can caravan to the hospital and then to my place for an evening of *Die Hard* on DVD.

The body is that of an elderly woman. She simply lied down on the icy grass and died. She's only wearing her blue fluffy slippers and purple satin nightgown. As we stand there, we hear people calling from not so far away.

"Grace? Grace, can you hear me?" a woman's voice echoes.

"Grace? Grace!" another voice calls, this time a man's.

It isn't long before the two people attached to the voices round the corner on the opposite side of the road. Their faces freeze in horror as they take in the scene. All of us standing around, the sheet pulled up over the dead woman's frost-covered body. The woman runs up to me, frantic.

"What happened? Is that Grace? Oh no, oh no, oh no!" She sobs and buries her head in the man's chest.

"We work at Spring Sunset Assisted Living just down that way," he says. "Grace must have slipped out during dinner. We've been looking everywhere for her. She has dementia, and she's wearing a purple nightgown..." His voice trails off.

"I'm sorry, but you need to talk to one of the detectives." I feel like such an asshole, but it's not my job to deliver news like that to anyone. I don't know what else to say to them. I'm genuinely sad that this is how Christmas is going to end for every one of us gathered here.

"She seemed like she was having such a good night. She even recognized her husband earlier in the day. She hasn't done that in weeks," the woman says, barely loud enough to be heard above the wind.

"It's okay, Mary. We'll figure out where she's being taken and then we'll tell her family," the man says, desperately trying to comfort her.

"She was alone! She died all alone in the cold, and it's my fault!"

I turn and start back to the van. I need to get as far away from all this misery as I can or I'm going to start fucking crying, and I don't want to cry. I watch from the back side of the van while the police get all the details from the assisted living employees.

Shrimp ramen, that's what flavor I choose for my dinner tonight. And *Die Hard*. I still have something to look forward to.

CHAPTER TWELVE

"Dad, that old guy is still out back in the parking garage! It's been like two weeks! I can smell him. The whole parking garage smells like him!"

"You should have taken him when I told you to," he says from behind his desk in the office.

"There's no way this is on me. You forgot he was back there, didn't you?"

"I didn't forget, I just haven't had time to take care of it. Now, you take him right now to the morgue downtown. They said I could store him there for a week or so until I can get the paperwork taken care of and get him cremated." Dad is so calm it's like he's talking about a casserole.

"This whole thing is so fucked up. He shouldn't even be here. You should never have said you would store him when we don't have a goddamn cooler." I storm out and slam the door to the office. I want to drive home my point of how annoying all this is. It's my Friday, so maybe after I take this old guy downtown the rest of my day will be easy. I'm excited to go to Punk Fest tomorrow. Joel scored us tickets. After that I have Hanukkah dinner with Dad and his wife. I'm not looking forward to that dinner at all. Maybe the music will be so loud it'll leave my ears ringing and I won't be able to hear my dad go on and on about shit I don't care about.

I drop the old man's body off and the rest of the day flies by with, surprisingly, no more dead bodies.

The next day, Joel picks me up bright and early.

"I got us a show! On New Year's Eve! At The Mantel Club! They're having an all-ages show that has like, fifteen bands on the bill. We're on at 6:30 p.m., but hey, it's a show!" Joel is so excited he can barely stand it.

"Awesome, man!"

"Also, Myrna is gonna come see us play and she's gonna bring her roommate. Her single roommate who has giant boobs and comes from a rich family."

"Okay. What's her name?"

"I don't know... Big boobs?" Joel laughs.

"What's going on with you and Myrna anyway? Are you guys official?"

"Yep, it's official. She's my special lady. She's five years older than me but I don't care. She's awesome. She reminds me of my mom."

"Gross, Joel!"

"She thinks what we do for work is cool. She doesn't think we're weirdos. She's mature."

They're such a weird couple. Myrna is a strait-laced hospital administrator who doesn't drink or smoke and has lots of cats. Joel believes in Bigfoot and only owns one pair of socks because he says the sock industry is just a racket.

We pull into the festival parking lot and the music is already pouring out into the mid-morning air. The air is crisp and cold, and everything smells like dirt and cigarettes. I don't recognize the band, but the music is super catchy. Once inside, we find the smoking area and share a joint. This is going to be an epic day.

Six hours later, my feet are freezing and soaked from the snow that's been falling on and off all day. My hands are bright red and burning. I'm half drunk, mostly stoned, starving, and sure enough, my ears are ringing like mad.

I thought of nothing all day but the music. Except when I had to take a piss. The Porta-Potty I stepped into was foul. There was a mountain of shit and toilet paper half frozen in the toilet. It smelled exactly like the YMCA bathroom I was at earlier in the week to pick up the body of a man who died in the showers. I got a flash of his naked body splayed out on the communal shower floor, covered in his own diarrhea because his bowels had released. I shake my head.

Stop it, stop it, stop it. Don't think about work, just listen to the drums. One, two, three, one, two, three... That's better.

We leave before the end of the show because I have to get to Dad's. Joel pulls up in front of my dad's house. I'm forty-five minutes late for Hanukkah dinner. I breathe into my palm to see if I stink of booze. I can't tell. I finish my cigarette and grab my coat from the back seat. I can't wait to eat. Meatballs are tradition for my family on holidays, and my mouth is watering just thinking about them.

"See you at work Monday."

"Are you sure you should go in there? I can take you home if you want, Dave."

"Nah, I'm good. See ya."

I walk up the long path to the front door and pause. Do I ring the bell or knock? Do I try the knob and just walk in like I'm not super late? Fuck it, that's what I'll do. If I slink in looking guilty I'll get shit, but maybe if I walk in and just ignore it I can power through the awkwardness.

I try the knob and it turns with no resistance. As the door opens, I hear lots of people chatting in the dining room. I step inside and the warmth washes over me in waves. The smell of food is intoxicating, and I follow it like a siren song deeper into the house and through to the kitchen. I round the corner of the kitchen and step into the dining room. No one notices me at first and I let out a sigh of relief. I see my empty spot at the table and make my way to it. I lower into my chair and reach out for a roll.

"Looks like his royal highness has finally decided to join us."

I look up and lock eyes with my dad. He doesn't drink, but his face is flushed red like he's been drinking all day.

"Sorry I'm late. I got...I got stuck in traffic." I survey the room. There are several couples I don't recognize sitting at the table looking at me. Important people from the synagogue or businesspeople, maybe. My half-brother who's a teenager sits in a chair at the head of the table. Fitting, since Dad treats him like the perfect son he always wanted while my brother and I are just the disappointments.

"Mort, have you met my son David?" Dad asks an older bald guy sitting across from me.

"No. It's nice to meet you, David," Mort says stiffly.

"Nice to meet you too," I say without making eye contact.

"David is the guy who pulled off that dead man's prosthetic legs a few weeks back when he tripped and fell," Dad gloats, staring straight at me as he states this for all to hear.

He knows this will push my buttons. Making me look like a child and a constant fuck up to all his friends is my dad's favorite pastime.

"At least I'm not the one who forgot a guy's arm at a scene," I mutter under my breath.

"What's that?"

"Nothing, Dad."

"David is also in love with one of the coroners. That weird, tall one at the general hospital with the face of a warthog and personality to match."

What the fuck? He just doesn't know when to stop. Why is it so important to him to make me look like a stupid asshole? Like yelling at me all week at work isn't enough, he has to amuse himself by teasing me. Are these old men he's invited here really impressed with the fact that he's picking on his adult son?

56

I look around and everyone except my dad looks uncomfortable. The whole room falls quiet. I will not take the bait. I'm just going to eat and then leave. I'm not going to fight with him on Hanukkah.

I take a bite of my roll and hope he'll change the subject.

"David did the same thing when he was a kid. He was twelve and we sent him off to summer camp. He had a crush on one of his camp counselors. She was also tall and kind of weird. You certainly have a type, don't you?" he laughs.

"It's Dave, not David," I say, sounding meek even to myself.

"I named you. I know what your name is."

I lift my head and look him straight in the eyes. I wish I could punch him in the face and make him shut the fuck up. I stand up and start to walk out.

"Where are you going? Look at that. I give him a job and a van and invite him over, even though he should be working, and this is the thanks I get? He walks out in the middle of dinner? Spoiled!"

I stop in the hallway and ball my fists. I want so much to punch the wall and call him a prick. I take a deep breath and step closer to the door. I will not make a scene. I will not stoop to his level. I will be the bigger man.

I grab the doorknob and fling the door open. I can still hear him bitching about me even this far away from the table. I slam the door and briskly walk toward my house in the bitter cold. Fuck him. I fucking hate him. I will not get sucked into this life and this shit show. I'm going to get the fuck out of this town and play music for a living. Fuck him.

CHAPTER THIRTEEN

Valentine's Day. Oh, Valentine's Day. I never really cared one way or another about this holiday. When I wake up, I have the weirdest thought: Paige likes chocolates. Maybe I should get her a box? But not today. I'll get it tomorrow when the candy goes on sale. That way she won't think I'm seriously trying to impress her.

The first call comes earlier than I expect. Usually if there's an incident on this holiday it comes later in the night, but this call comes in at 6:30 p.m.

Joel and I pull up to the apartment building we're sent to, not sure what to expect. Dad didn't think to give us any details. The apartment building looks normal enough, one in a line of many other identical ones on the block. It's a four story building with a red brick facade and a small walkway. There are two generic shrubs planted on either side of the front door. It feels more like walking into some anonymous medical building than where people live. There's no warmth or signs of life.

We enter the building lobby with the stretcher and hear the anguished wails of a sobbing woman in the hall outside an apartment. The building echoes with the decorative ghosts of its better days: the nineties. There are no windows or paintings in the lobby, just a long line of mailboxes set into the wall on the left, and thick, dark green carpet running the length of the hallway to the elevator. The ceilings are lined with fluorescent light fixtures, some of the bulbs burned out or flickering.

"I can't live here anymore! I can't! Not after what he did!"

An officer tries to calm the woman, but she isn't listening. She's frail and thin. She shakes violently with every sob. Her blonde hair is pulled into a tight bun on top of her head. Her big blue eyes spill tears all over her silk blouse. She seems a tad dramatic in her reaction to whatever is on the other side of her door, but pretty girls can be dramatic.

A tall young guy has his arms wrapped around her in an effort to comfort, and she's on the verge of collapsing into them. His greasy blonde hair hangs in his eyes and stares at the ground, rubbing the tips of his loafers together nervously. He looks like a kid. I wonder what he's thinking?

We walk in and find it's a regular old apartment. Nothing but IKEA decor and Target wall art. A TV, a couch, and a coffee table.

"He's in the back here, guys."

We make our way further into the apartment, past a Pepto-Bismol-pink bathroom, to the bedroom. There, naked on the bed, is the body.

"So… What? The boyfriend died while they were banging?" I ask the cop filling out paperwork.

"Not quite."

That's when I notice the blood spray that covers the headboard and track it all the way up the wall to the textured ceiling. Bits of brain and skull splatter the wall where the words THIS IS YOUR FAULT are scrawled in black marker. Brutal.

We load up and my phone rings. Another call, another stop. Except this time we're headed to a small house on the east side of the city. Might as well grab this second body before dropping off the first and save myself some time. It's a homicide, and the coroner is already there so at least there won't be any waiting around. Just in and out, bag and tag.

The house is a small white bungalow with no parking in front on the busy street, so I block the neighbors' driveway. Fuck it. We'll be quick.

In the frigid February darkness it's hard to make out any details carved in the wooden dormers or the woodwork on the deck handrail, but once the door opens and the crime scene lights hit, I can see small birds lovingly carved into the wood all over the front of the house. It's like a gingerbread house.

Joel and I take the backup stretcher we keep in the van and head inside.

We stand in the living room while James finishes telling the lead detective about how he went to a Comic-Con last week and hooked up with a Lara Croft lookalike. The detective shrugs, either because he doesn't know who Lara Croft is, or more likely because he doesn't care.

James rolls his eyes and turns to us with a smile.

"Happy Valentine's Day, boys!"

"It will be when I get off work and buy my special lady friend a box of pink wine and some cinnamon rolls." Joel's excitement is palpable.

"It's supposed to be chocolates and red wine, dude. Everyone knows that."

"Nah Dave, a real woman likes a nice pink wine and a hearty pastry."

"Fear not, boys," James says. "This call will leave you feeling a little less romantic."

"The last one was a Valentine's suicide. Does it top that?"

"You'll see. She's in the bedroom." James motions us down the hall.

We walk through the living room and down the hall. Whoever this woman is, she has horrible taste in music. One glance at the rack of CDs in her foyer and you know that she loves sappy love songs from the seventies. Some of the worst music in the history of the world was written in the seventies, and this woman has all the classics: sappy disco, horrible pop. Anne Murray.

The weird thing is that she can't be more than thirty. At least, not according to the pictures hanging in the kitchen. She's young—too young to settle on a single genre of music. Her home is filled with mismatched furniture, the kind of place you live in college. There's a coffee table made from a piece of wood and some milk crates, and a papasan chair with pillows that lost their fluffiness long ago.

It goes without saying that a person's life is more than the sum of their things and their terrible taste in music, but you can still get a general idea how they lived by the things they surrounded themselves with. This woman seems young.

She's splayed out naked on the bed. Weird. Is that a Valentine's Day thing? Both her breasts are cut off. Her eyes are wide open with the last moments of pain frozen on her face. An extension cord is wrapped tightly around her neck. It's knotted awkwardly on the side so the knot rests against her cheek. I can only hope for her sake that her breasts were removed post-mortem. One breast sits on a record that's skipping on the record player on in the corner. The other breast seems to have vanished. Written on the wall in lipstick are the words THANKS FOR THE MAMMARIES.

What a fucking asshole thing to do. What wannabe serial killer bullshit is this? Why does it piss me off so bad? I look over at Joel and he doesn't seem bothered at all. He's just getting the body bag ready like it's no big deal. Like she's not laying here with her tits missing.

"Want to get a bite to eat after this?"

"I don't really have an appetite after this, Joel."

"What do you mean?"

"I mean this is fucking gross, and wrong, and it makes me sick to my stomach!"

"How is this worse than the last one?" Joel seems genuinely confused.

"It just fucking is. I don't know." *Fuck!* What is wrong with me? My phone rings again. Fuck, fuck, fuck!

"Death by natural causes. Just an old man. Get it done quick and you can head home after."

CHAPTER FOURTEEN

We stop at the morgue to drop off the two bodies. Joel and I each take a stretcher and head inside. I wonder if Paige is in the office. I mean, I don't really give a shit, but maybe she's wearing some holiday outfit I can make fun of, or something… Why the fuck do I keep thinking about Paige? Why did that mutilated woman upset me so much? Am I losing my ability to stay unemotional? My stomach rumbles. Maybe if I eat something I'll feel better. Am I getting depressed?

Third call of Valentine's day, third body. Another non-descript apartment building. I'm not really paying attention anymore. Anyway, I keep thinking about…Paige. *Why?* Do I actually like that shiksa giraffe? I mean, she's easy to look at and easier to talk to. Shit, I do like her. Shit. But she's so damn annoying!

Walking into the room, I realize no one around me is doing anything. They're all staring at the body.

He's a man of around eighty, perched on the edge of his La-Z-Boy chair with his feet positioned on the edge of a small coffee table. Right in front of himself he's placed a large mirror, balanced on the table so it's pointing right back at him. He's naked with his knees pointed out past his elbows, hands clenching his limp dick, his shaved asshole on full display. This is how he died: in the middle of jerking off while watching himself and sticking things in his ass. I can tell that's the top of a carrot peeking out of his asshole.

His apartment is immaculate. It's well cared for, with items that are clearly valuable to him. His furniture is pristine, as though no one has sat on it since the moment it entered the room. The walls are covered with paintings by surrealist artists, which is somewhat unnerving because my mom's house is covered in some of the same pieces of artwork. The drapes are clean and pulled back, letting in tons of natural light. This, overall, would be a perfect real estate listing for prospective buyers. Remodeled bathroom, shaker cabinets in the kitchen, and the corpse of an old man with a carrot hanging out of his exposed rectum, bathed in afternoon light.

So that's what we walk in to. We stand around taking in the scene for a bit. Me, Joel, and four cops, when in walks Paige. She's wearing a holiday outfit, just like I thought she might. A hot pink blouse with white pants. Why would you wear white pants to a scene? Is she insane? She wears a sparkly headband with two glittery hearts on springs that swing back and forth when she moves her head. Her dark curly hair swings wild and free around her face, which is still the color of skim milk. I have to stop staring at her before she realizes what I myself realized just a few moments ago.

"This guy's balls are swollen like crazy. Seriously!" Joel stammers.

I feel sick again. Paige doesn't look amused either.

"Joel. Seriously?"

"I'm not sure we can pick him up without those things popping like giant zits," Joel says, and he's right.

The old man's balls are swollen to the size of little watermelons and bulging as if waiting for the perfect moment to pop and rain semen, blood, and who knows what other kind of putrid moisture, down on all of our heads. His balls are swollen because he's been sitting in that chair, slowly decomposing for the last eighteen or so hours, Paige guesses. Biology can be a cruel mistress.

"I do not want to fucking do this," I say. I just don't have it in me. On top of the horrors of today, my roommate showed up last night with yet another fucking cat, bringing the household total to six. Six cats. Six shitting, shedding, scratching, monster assholes. I fucking hate cats. I lost my debit card sometime between last night and this morning—god knows where—and my fucking coffee dumped in my lap, soaking my brand-new pack of smokes at the kitchen table before I was even fully awake. All of these normal, everyday things that hadn't been a big deal earlier pile on to all the horrible and disgusting things I've seen today. I'm in a foul mood.

Joel can tell it's best if he makes the first move. He knows me well enough to know I'm past the point of aggravation and heading toward a total toddler-style meltdown. He decides for once to grab the top half, leaving me to take the lighter load. It's nice of him, except that to grab the lower half I'll have to bend down and get my face way too close to this guy's ticking time bomb of a nut sack.

"No way, man. I want the top half."

Without arguing, Joel slowly puts down the arms and quietly make his way around to the front of the chair. He's face to face with the thing we've all avoided making eye contact with since entering the apartment: this old man's clean-shaven asshole.

It's oddly hairless. I mean, it's clear that he has to perform some sort of hair removal in order to get it that clean. He has large white tufts of hair growing in clumps all over his wrinkled, spotted, withered body. Everywhere except his pink, disgusting asshole.

"Maybe it's a home wax job?" offers one of the cops.

"No way he did that himself, man. Look at his toenails. They're talons the color of movie popcorn butter! If he can't cut his own toenails, how the hell did he manage to reach around and wax his asshole so well?" asks the other cop.

"Well, he does have the whole mirror thing down. Maybe he just got better at it over time," adds Joel.

"That's so weird that a man would take so much care in preparing his rectum for whatever the hell he has jammed in it, but make no attempt to wax his back, trim his ear hair, or even shave the top of his nose. I just don't get it," says Paige.

I look at her, shocked that she's chiming in. It snaps me out of my funk for a second, because she's right. I crack a smile at her, and she cocks her head to one side and smiles back. Shit. Now she knows. It's probably written all over my face right now. Goddamnit. Okay, maybe she doesn't know. She's friendly. Maybe she's just being friendly.

"Well either way, it was clearly a point of pride for him. At least he went out doing what he loved, with his fancy, hairless asshole on display for all to comment on."

That makes her laugh, and her laugh sounds like pure happiness as it echoes through the room.

Everyone watches as Joel and I maneuver our stretcher, figuring out the path of least resistance to load the old man into his body bag. No way am I risking putting him on the stretcher with just a sheet over him. He's going in a bag.

We approach his body as a SWAT team would approach a bomb: with precision, stealth movements, and patience. We manage to get him gently onto the stretcher and into the waiting body bag. As we start to zip the bag, Joel suddenly and violently sneezes. We collectively gasp as his spasming body lurches forward and slams into the gurney. All at once the dead man lets out the most god-awful corpse moan, making all of us jump. It doesn't happen all the time, but it's not uncommon either for a corpse to groan or moan when it's jostled. It has to do with all the gases that fill the body cavity. He can't fart or burp to release the gas, so seeing as it must come out one end or another, it ends up being the mouth because that is an easier path than all the way down through this man's already-crowded rectum.

"What the hell! Is there a bird in here? I'm allergic to birds! There better not be a bird in here or my eyes are going to swell shut! I didn't see any bird cages!" Joel shrieks, suddenly panicked.

"I don't know, man. I don't see any birds."

"That's so weird. That only happens around birds. Doesn't matter if it's a parakeet or an eagle, they make my whole head swell up! Something with the dander I'm allergic to." Joel frantically scratches his entire body.

I finish zipping up the black plastic body bag and head for the door. If there is a goddamn bird in here, Joel will manage to make me do all the work of loading this guy in while he waits in the van with his EpiPen.

We gently push the gurney down the hall and out the door toward the elevator, avoiding any and all bumps possible. Once in the elevator, Joel lets out one more body-shaking sneeze and from somewhere inside that goddamn bag of horrors, we hear it: a very distinctive *pop*. We hold our breaths as the elevator descends, waiting to see if anything is going to leak from the bag. Seconds tick by, with no dripping or seepage.

"That's it. I hate this day. Valentine's Day is dead to me," I declare.

CHAPTER FIFTEEN

It's been a few months since our New Year's Eve show went well. We got lots of laughs from the six people that watch our set. We now have a solid two albums worth of songs. We just need to record them and we'll be set.

There aren't words to describe how good it feels to play music. Mostly about silly shit, but that's the whole point. Nothing too serious. Nothing that requires too much thought. I *love* the feeling of playing a character, of being someone else completely when I'm on stage.

I'm not the Dave who was jumped by neo-Nazis in high school and got the shit kicked out of him. I'm not the guy who everyone says wet his bed at Hebrew camp. I didn't. I took a nap after swimming without changing out of my swim shorts, but there was no convincing anyone after that asshole Samuel spread the word. I'm not weird Dave who picks up bodies. I'm a guy in a band. I'm a musician. I'm important, and I'm finally starting to feel happy.

"We got offered a tour! I mean, it's a little one, and it's only with one other band, but hey, we got offered a fucking tour, dude!" Joel bounces off the walls with excitement. "We're going to have to convince your dad to let us both have the time off, though."

"Shit. He's never going to go for that, especially if I tell him what it's for."

"Doesn't he know you're a musician now, not bound to the rules of mainstream society?"

"I told him, but I know he wasn't really listening because when I got done telling him he said 'did you go out and talk to Ed at the old cemetery in Eastland like I asked you to? We could use some extra business from them', and I just let it go after that."

"Dude, fuck that shit. We're going. It's five shows in seven days. Technically we could come home every night after each show, but it would be so much more fun to be on the road. The other band has a van we can ride in."

"What is the other band?"

"They play covers of old girl group songs from the fifties, but in a punk rock style. They're called Sock Hop Slaughter."

"Weird, but whatever. Let's make it happen!"

The next day I approach my dad and ask for the time off. He does exactly what I expect him to do: he laughs at me.

"No. You can't take a week off with the guy I would have cover your shifts. Besides, I need you to go to that conference on the east coast for the NFDA."

"But Dad, I've never taken vacation before and I've never even called in sick. Henry will be fine without us. Or even if you just give me evenings off, I can work during the day or something. This is important to me. Please. We can make it work."

"No. It might be important to you, but you know what's important to me? My clients."

"Even more important than the happiness of your son?"

"Yes."

He says it so devoid of emotion that I know he'll never budge. I walk out of his office feeling lower than I have in a long time. With one word my hopes are squashed. I knew it was a long shot, but he said it so plainly. He doesn't give a shit what's important to me.

I sit outside the office in my van and light a cigarette while dialing Joel. "He said no, dude."

"What?"

"I told you he would. We're never going to be able to tour." I can tell he hears the resignation in my voice. There's a long pause between us.

"Well, fuck. Just because we can't do the tour doesn't mean we can't play the show here on the first night, right?"

"That's true, I guess."

"Well, that's better than nothing, isn't it? And besides, there will be other tours with other bands. Don't let your dad steal your dreams and piss all over them."

"You're right, Joel. This can still be fun."

"Maybe you can write a song and debut it at the show. One about how much your dad sucks."

"That I can definitely do. Thanks, man."

"It'll be fine. See ya tomorrow."

"See ya."

I'm surprised that Joel's words actually cheer me up. He's right. I'm not going to give up just because we hit one roadblock. Shit, we're just starting out, and we have all the time in the world to go on tour.

I start the van and shift into reverse, ready to back out of the driveway. I pause for a moment and flick the butt of my cigarette at the office trailer defiantly. My dad hates that I smoke, and he hates cigarette butts even more. Fuck him. I jam my hand out the window and give him the finger, even though he can't see me through the closed blinds. It still feels good.

CHAPTER SIXTEEN

The National Funeral Directors Conference is held once a year, and it's like going to Disneyland for my dad. He looks forward to it all year and always goes alone so he feels like he's on vacation, since he never actually takes one. This year I'm going in his place. Not because he doesn't want to go, but because his wife insisted that he stay home for my half-brother's bar mitzvah. He didn't come to mine because he was working.

"Listen, David. When you check in to the conference on the first day, make sure to get to the hall right when they open. I signed you up to get your cremation certification, and that starts right at 9 a.m."

"Why did you do that? I don't want to do cremations."

"It won't be long before you start doing more on the funeral directing side, and you might as well get certified. Plus, I get a huge discount if you do it at the show instead of locally."

There it is. He's always trying to spend the least amount of money possible.

"I need you to find me a new vendor for all my basic supplies. The most important thing is they have to be cheaper than the place I use now. I wrote a list of all the things I get from them with prices, so find a place that carries the same stuff. Maybe one that gets their stuff from China. That's always cheaper."

I start to answer him, but he cuts me off.

"And I don't want a place that wants payment up front. Make sure they have a sixty or ninety day overlap in billing."

"How am I supposed to find out if the company does that?"

"Just do it. I like having a little wiggle room when it comes to paying vendors."

"Okay, but since I'll be in Toronto for four days, I'm going to see some live music. There's a club out there that bands always make sure to play because it's legendary."

"You're not doing that. I need you to network and go to the dinners and hob-knob with all the other funeral big-wigs. Your days and nights are booked with things for work. You have to learn how to do this stuff if you're going to take over for me when I retire."

"Dad, you can't expect me to spend all my free time with these funeral people. I want to go do my own shit, too. I've never been out east on my own." The disappointment starts to set in. I have so many things planned. I've been checking venues and seeing what kinds of shows will be going on, and if there are any open mics. I want to try out this new idea I have for a solo acoustic thing, and there's no better place to try it than in a different city with people I never have to see again if I bomb. I haven't told Joel because I don't want him to freak out that I'm breaking up the band, but I have some ideas that would be better done on my own. I've been learning how to play the guitar for a few weeks now, on the weekends and my days off. I figure I only need a few chords and I'll be good. That's the beauty of punk rock.

"Did you hear me? You're not even listening, goddamnit!"

"Yes, I heard you. You said you couldn't book a direct flight, so I have some layovers."

"Whatever you do, do not miss your connecting flights. There are four of them."

"*Four?* It's only six hours from Vancouver to Toronto. Why do I have four connections?"

"Because it was a hundred dollars cheaper. You'll fly Vancouver to Boulder, Boulder to Detroit, Detroit to Calgary, Calgary to Toronto."

"What the fuck? I have to go into the States? That means I have to go through customs twice! How long is my travel day?" I'm freaking out. I fucking hate flying! How could he do this to me?

"With layovers and time changes, it's about twelve hours total."

"No fucking way! You know I hate flying! All to save a hundred bucks? Fuck, Dad, take that money out of my paycheck instead of this bullshit!"

"Hey! Don't curse at me! Just do as you're told and get this shit figured out! The only reason you're not flying standby—which is even cheaper—is because I need you there for that certification."

He shoves a pile of papers at me in a flimsy blue folder. Panic floods my body, and I shake. I'm terrified of flying. I have this awful nightmare when I have to travel where the plane crashes and my arms are ripped off. Then I drown because we crash into the ocean and I can't swim because my fucking arms are gone. Every time it's the same damn nightmare, so at least I know what's in store for me tonight.

I slam the door of the office on my way out. The trailer shakes. I've started doing it every time I leave a meeting with my dad. I hate this job. I hate this goddamn job. I don't want to get certified in cremation. I want to quit and go on tour.

I climb into the driver's seat of my van and flip through the papers he gave me. There's a handwritten list on top: hazmat suits, arm and hand positioners, restorative wax and spatulas, plastic underwear, absorbent cavity pads, body inserts, and orifice guards. Great. This expo is going to be a fucking nightmare. I haven't given a thought to what it's really going to consist of until this very moment. I've been thinking of it as a paid trip to Toronto. Now I have to find a vendor for fucking cavity pads? I can only imagine what those fucking things look like, let alone what they do.

Travel day comes and I make sure I'm at the airport an hour early for my flight. That means I'm there at 4:30 a.m. I have a carry-on duffle bag and a garment bag for the itchy wool suit I borrowed from Dad.

As I wander through the airport to my terminal, there's not a single restaurant or store open. I'm starving, but there isn't anything I can do about it now. I grab a bottle of water, a Coke, a bag of cashews, and some Red Vines. All of that will go nicely with the Xanax my mom gave me for the anxiety.

I find my terminal and hunker down in the middle of a row of uncomfortable chairs that are bolted to the floor. It smells like Lysol and the flickering fluorescent lights hurt my head. The flight boards on time, and I'm off.

The day is a blur of shitty airplane snacks and uncomfortable naps in tiny mid-row seats. The familiar terror and nerves overtake me with each take-off and return with each landing. It's night by the time I land in Toronto, and all I want is a decent meal and my feet on the ground.

I pick up my rental car and head for the hotel. It sounds like a fancy one—The Regent—but based on my flights, I have no faith that my dad would put me up someplace decent. To my surprise, the hotel isn't as bad as I imagine it might be. It's a non-descript room with generic furniture, a view of the parking lot, and free drip coffee in the lobby. The smell of chlorine from the indoor pool permeates the first floor. I should've brought a swimsuit.

My exhausted body collapses on the bed and I'm out almost instantly. I fall into a fitful sleep with nightmares of rotting corpses shopping in a Costco warehouse, trying to find the aisles filled with cavity cement and plastic underwear. I toss and turn until I can't stand it anymore and flip on the light. I'm jet lagged, and as soon as I open my eyes, I want to shut them again and collapse back into sleep. I'm confused, but it's only 3 a.m. I watch some CNN and eventually fall back asleep to the sound of the reporter's voice. This time there are no nightmares.

I roll over and open my eyes, feeling well rested. I lay for a moment, rehashing all the instructions I was given for my first day of the conference. I rub my eyes and check the clock. 3:27. Is it p.m. or a.m.? Shit, it's p.m. I slept for twelve hours? *Shit!* I missed everything! I missed the certification and the meet and greets. *Fuck!*

I frantically shower and shove myself into the ill-fitting wool suit. It's about three inches too short and four inches too wide for me. I look like a kid playing dress-up. I check the itinerary Dad set up for me. I should be testing for my cremation certification right now. So much for that. At 5 p.m. is the Funeral Directors Under Forty dinner. Maybe I can get a decent meal there.

CHAPTER SEVENTEEN

The dinner for Funeral Directors Under Forty is exactly what I thought it would be. In the hall where the dinner is being held there's a sea of young professionals dressed and ready for the corporate world. People fill their plates at the all-you-can-eat buffet and others stand in line at the open bar. There are groups of people chatting and tables filled with people happily munching away on their dinner.

The buffet smells amazing and I realize how hungry I am. The Xanax and Red Vines from the previous day left me running on empty, so I head for the buffet and grab a plate. The buffet reminds me of something you would find on a casino boat. There's a carving station with roast beef and turkey, a sushi spread, pasta, soups, and salad. Waiters and cooks shuffle away the dirty plates and empty trays, replacing them with clean dishes and freshly piled trays.

I load my plate with salmon sushi rolls and hunks of roast beef. I grab two rolls and a large Coke and scan the room for an empty table. I spot one in the far corner of the room. I don't feel like making small talk with strangers, I just want to stuff myself silly. I settle at the table and dig in. No one tries to sit with me. No one even seems to notice I'm there, which is just the way I like it.

Three plates later, I feel the pangs of regret and overindulgence. Why did I eat so much? I feel awful and think of going back to my room for the night, but damn it, I'm going to enjoy myself while I'm here.

Back at the room, I change into my regular clothes and head for the venue. I just need to lose myself in the music of the night and have a few drinks. That will make me feel normal again and help shake off my impending food coma.

I walk into The Kathedral and immediately hit a wall of loud, unruly music. It makes my ears ring and my chest thump. It's glorious. I spend the next four hours reveling in the release and distraction. I befriend some crusty punks. We drink and talk music.

"I do this dirty, comedic, acoustic punk thing," I tell one of them. I've been struggling to describe what I've been working on over the last few weeks alone in my room.

"Cool, cool, man. You got any shows coming up?"

"Nah, not yet. I'm just starting out."

"Well, if you're ever out this way again and need a show, hit me up. I'll give you my email. I book a club in Hamilton that always needs bands."

This is it. This is the networking I need to be doing. Not finding people to sell my dad cheaper orifice cleaner. It feels as natural as putting on my shoes. I feel alive and excited thinking about coming back out here on tour. Is it really this easy? You just meet people at shows, get to talking, and that's it? Now I have a connection.

I make my way back to the hotel in a drunken haze. I walk, rather than drive. It's not too far. The night air is so clean and I'm riding a high, imagining the possibilities of a life on the road, making records, selling merch, meeting new people wherever I go. I can start my real life. One that I choose. When I get home, I'm going to quit. I'm still young, and it's not too late. I don't have to do anything I don't want to do. I'm fucking done.

I wake up the next day with a massive throbbing in my head and churning in my guts. My angry resolve to quit my job has evaporated. I crawl out from under the covers to look at the clock. 7:30 a.m. It's my day to wander the expo floor, and I'm supposed to attend a lecture on liability in the cemetery to learn about cemetery legal issues. After that, I'm going back to see another punk show at The Kathedral.

I shower and put the wool suit back on, avoiding the mirror on my way to get breakfast, mostly because I don't want to see myself looking like my dad. I grab a continental breakfast of dry mini-muffins and a few sad pieces of limp, undercooked bacon, then head to the convention.

The giant expo hall is dizzying. Every direction I look there are row after row of booths. My eyes go fuzzy and I can't focus on a thing. There's a sea of people pushing from one booth to another, slowly ushering me down the aisles. I feel like one of those fish that ride the current from one part of the ocean to another.

Ethical urns, funeral financing, grief counseling, electronic guestbooks... The list of vendors is never-ending. I never thought there were this many companies powering the funeral industry.

I stop at one booth, a company that sells body coolers. I think of the old man in the parking area at the cemetery. Maybe if I can get a good deal on a body cooler, my dad might forget I missed the cremation certification. There are pictures of coolers of all sizes hanging from the dividing curtains. There's one cooler on display and it fills most of the booth. The salespeople are all busy talking to other conference-goers, which is kind of a relief. I don't feel like talking. I glance at the price tag. $12,999 with a long red slash through it, and a new price of $9,999 written below.

"Are you in the market for a new cooling system?"

I turn and see an older man coming toward me, his bald head and belly reminding me of my grandfather.

"Not really. Just looking, thanks."

"Well you know, I've been in this business a long time, and if there's one thing you'll need more than any other it's a good, reliable cooler."

"I don't have the authority to buy things for the business. I'm just here to check things out." That seems like a nice easy way to get away from the salesman.

"I was your age when I started," he says, smiling. "I spent my whole life doing different jobs in the business. Working my way up. You play your cards right and you'll be set for life in this industry."

Set for life. *Set for life.* It feels like a death sentence hanging in the air between us. I picture myself in ten years. Twenty. Thirty. Would I end up like this guy? Could I stomach an entire lifetime working with death? Always so painfully aware of the eternal countdown we're all trying to outrun?

Panic sets in. I have to get away from him. From this whole place. I can feel my throat beginning to close and my face flush. "Have a good day," I manage to squeak as I head for the exit doors. The cool air hits me and I breathe again. My arms tingle and my vision gets fuzzy. I sit on the curb and put my head between my legs.

Just breathe. Focus on breathing.

I'm done for today. I need to feel something familiar and comforting. I head to my car and leave for the hotel, stopping at a Wendy's for dinner. This feels normal, like home. A giant cheeseburger and fries, not some fancy piece of salmon on a white plate surrounded by a sauce that's dribbled in a quirky design.

I spend the next two days sleeping during the day and drinking at The Kathedral at night. I've turned this into my own kind of vacation. When I get home, my dad will most likely fire me. That would be such a relief.

For the journey home, Dad's booked me a direct flight. It almost makes me feel bad for doing such a shit job at the conference. I drink tiny bottles of alcohol and sleep, trying not to think too much about the inevitable fight we're going to have.

CHAPTER EIGHTEEN

I've been sitting at my dad's dining room table for the past ten minutes. He sits across from me, silent and red-faced with rage.

"What *exactly* did you do while you were in Toronto?" he asks.

"I went to the expo."

"No, you didn't. You didn't get your cremation certification, you didn't go to the golf tournament, you didn't find me a vendor, and you didn't network. So, what did you do?"

"I found a vendor who sells coolers. We could use one, if you're going to keep telling people we have one."

"Don't change the subject. I don't want a goddamn cooler. I want to know what you did while you were wasting all my money. I paid for your flight, your hotel, and your rental car, and you're going to pay back every penny of that." His anger hangs thick in the air. His arms shake. Clearly, he wants to reach out and choke me.

"Look, I don't think this is the job for me. I think you should just fire me and call it done. I tried, and it didn't work."

"Ha! I'm not going to fire you! You're going to work off what you owe me, and then you're going to pay for your own cremation certification."

"No, I'm not. I hate this goddamn job and I don't want it." Now my anger is rising.

"You can't quit unless I say so, and you are not quitting. Now go home, take the rest of the night off, and get your ass to work tomorrow morning."

"You're not listening, Dad! I said I quit!"

"And I said I'll see you tomorrow! Now get out of my house!"

What the fuck? How am I not making this clear? He doesn't get to say I don't fucking quit!

He sits, glaring at me.

"I'm done."

"Here's the deal, David. You are my son. You work for me. I *own* you. You'll pick up bodies for a few more years, then you'll get your funeral director's license, and then I will sell you the company. End of discussion. Get the fuck out of my house."

This is going in circles. I stand and walk out of the room, straight out the front door. I hear him cursing me under his breath, but I don't care. I slam the door behind me with the steadfast resolve that I will be sleeping in tomorrow. When I don't show, he'll know I'm serious. No one can force a person to work.

The next morning, the realities of being unemployed hit me as I lay in bed, swearing to myself that I'm not going in. I've been planning on buying a new guitar and drum kit soon. Recording costs a ton, plus there's gas to get to shows, and marketing. A music career has a ton of up-front costs. If I spend a few more weeks in this job, I'll be able to pay for all that and have money left over. Shit. The ends justify the means. If I want to have any chance at freedom, I need cash. I'll job hunt, and as soon as I find something better, I'll quit.

I get out of bed, make some coffee, hit the shower, and get dressed. I sit in the driveway while the van warms up and listen to the radio. A contest for two free tickets to the hockey game is starting and I listen closely to the question.

"What team has won the most Stanley Cups in the NHL to date?"

I know this! The Montreal Canadiens. I grab my phone and dial. It rings right away, against all odds, and the DJ answers. He asks again, and I shout "Montreal Canadiens!"

"That's right! Congratulations! You've won the tickets, now hold the line."

What a glorious moment! Maybe today is going to be a lucky one. I give the show's producer my info and she tells me to pick up the tickets at the Will Call window at the arena tonight.

As soon as I hang up, my phone rings again. It's Henry.

"Bad news. We need all hands on deck. We have a family of six we need transported. Carbon monoxide poisoning. I bet the furnace was clogged," Henry says.

"Fuck. Okay, text me the address. I'll be there."

I snap out of my happiness and back to reality. The game is tonight, too late to find someone to cover me. My only hope is that no one will die in the three-hour window of the game. It starts at 5 p.m. so maybe I'll get lucky again and it'll be a slow day.

Henry and I hustle to clear the family from their home and in no time flat we get everyone out and to the morgue. Sitting in the office we finally get some downtime to chat.

"What the hell happened in Toronto? Did you get arrested or something? Your dad's been in a foul mood and all he'll say is that you're in a shitload of trouble."

"No, nothing happened."

"Well something must have happened. Your dad keeps calling me dipshit and biting my head off every time I ask him a question."

"I mean, I missed my cremation certification, but that was because he booked me on these fucked up connecting flights and I had jet lag."

"All I know is if he's pissed at you, he needs to take it out on you. Not the rest of us. If he keeps up with the dipshit talk, I'm gonna pop him in the mouth."

Great. Now they all know it's my fault my dad is on a rampage. At least Joel won't hate me. He doesn't even notice when people are pissed at him, that's how little he cares.

In the middle of watching an episode of *Jerry Springer* with James in the morgue office—something we get to do when it's slow—Henry's phone rings. Another body needs transporting. Dad's avoiding calling me, so he just calls Henry. I'm fine with that.

We pull up to a boarding house at 1:14 p.m. There's only a few hours until the game and I'm not sure what to expect other than a man has hanged himself. It's a shabby old house with wilted camellias planted around a dead lawn that's scattered with dog shit, gleaming white in the sun. Mummified chunks of kibble diarrhea stare me in the face and it seems like an omen.

The thing about a hanging is that most people don't actually succeed in killing themselves quickly or efficiently. They suffocate because it's so hard to break your own neck, and it takes a long time to choke to death.

Hanging bodies are easy. Thirty minutes tops, in and out. I can still make the game.

I dodge the awkward mismatched furniture and sobbing housemates on my way down to the basement. What is that smell? Not decomp, thank god. It's more of a garlic cloud hanging in the air. Mm, garlic. Damn it, now I want Greek food. Kebabs with garlic sauce sounds delicious. Maybe this guy will be naked so we won't have to take the extra time to go through his pockets for personal items. Hopefully we can just cut him down and he'll slump right onto the stretcher. Done and done, and dinner time for me. Today just might work out after all. Everything's coming up Dave.

The dead guy, skinny and in his mid-twenties, is in full rigor. He isn't naked, which means we have to search his pockets. He's wearing all these horrible hemp necklaces and rings, which I never look forward to taking off of a stiff. We do it as a favor to the local cops since they all get skeeved out at the thought of touching a dead body.

Since I'm the taller of the two, it's up to me to cut him down while Henry gets the stretcher ready and prepares to catch him. The room has a bunch of exposed pipes running through the ceiling. It's clearly part of an unfinished basement that the owner broke up into several small rooms. There's exposed drywall and no windows. The dead man has hung himself from the exposed pipes, and lucky for everyone, he's maybe 110 lbs. Otherwise it would have snapped the pipe and flooded the basement.

He's hanging from a set of shoelaces and it's easy to cut him down. I expect to hear a thump as the last thread of the cord snaps, but instead all I heard is Henry.

"Nice! What are the chances of that?"

The space is small and the body is in full rigor. He's swinging a mere four inches above the ground. When I cut him down, he simply lands on his feet, standing straight up.

Henry giggles, and with a weird look on his face, he grabs the guy and starts to slow dance with him. "Check it out! This guy can still dance!"

I hear footsteps coming down the stairs and turn in time to see Paige. As she rounds the corner she freezes and her eyes grow wide in horror as what she's seeing starts to register. There's Henry, slow dancing with a dead body while humming "Moon River".

"Hey Paige, wanna dance?" Henry screeches in a high-pitched voice.

She shifts from startled to amused. She quickly tries to gather her composure and regain her professional facade.

"Don't be like that, Paige. I'm a good dancer, see!" Henry screeches as the dead man in a falsetto voice. He tries to make the guy dance and shimmy, but because he's stiff as a board, it looks more like he's just shaking the guy around like a piñata, trying to make all the candy fall out of him.

"Did you just *Weekend at Bernie's* me with a dead man?" she asks.

Henry doubles over with laughter. "Come on, it's funny! Right Dave?" Henry screeches.

"Don't bring me into this. I want no part of it."

"Oh, come on guys, don't you like my dancing?" Henry screeches again.

"Just get him on the stretcher. I want to go get lunch." I stifle a chuckle.

It's not standard practice to use a dead person as a puppet to elicit laughs from others, but today it's a much-needed break in the tension of the day.

"You'd better hope no one but us saw you do that," says Paige, trying hard to erase her smile.

"Eh. I'm sure he wouldn't mind," Henry says as we wrangle the body onto the stretcher.

"Still, be careful," Paige says. She turns to me and gives me a little wink. Her eyes are huge today and caked in purple sparkly eyeshadow. I can't stop the smile that spreads across my face. We both enjoy being in the moment with each other.

CHAPTER NINETEEN

The countdown to the night's hockey game continues. At 2:27 p.m. Henry and I climb the stairs of an old building. It used to be a decadent hotel in the nineteen-twenties but is now a horrible mess of an apartment building. None of the windows are open and no one is in the hallway. Not one person is curious enough to poke their head out to see what's going on. There are cats, though. Cats roam every inch of the hall. Meows, purring, and tumbleweeds of cat hair surround us. Maybe only cats live here. There's no elevator, so we climb two flights of stairs. There, at the top, is the stiff.

The dead man's head is caught in the wrought iron railing that should have been replaced decades ago. His body is wrapped at an impossible angle around it and lays crumpled on the top stair. I can't seem to make sense of how his body got so twisted up.

"Someone probably made him put his head in the railing, then they beat him with a sledgehammer, leaving him like this. Broken neck, bent and smashed up body, shattered legs," says James.

"Damn, that's brutal."

"Yep. And now I have to wait for the fire department to get here and cut the railing before I can finish the paperwork," says James.

"You sound irritated."

"Two words, Dave: cat shit. Have you bothered to look down at what we're standing on? It's everywhere!"

He isn't kidding. There's so much of it on the carpet, I mistakenly thought the carpet itself was brown. It's actually bright green underneath, once the toe of my shoe manages to chip away a bit of the pile beneath me. As I stand kicking at the hardened poop, Henry moves into a position where we can access the body. Before he's able to get even two steps away, he slips in fresh cat feces. Like a teenager on a slip and slide in the middle of summer, Henry elegantly falls and lands on his back, smearing himself with cat shit in the process. He lays there for a second, knowing that any hasty attempts to get up could lead to an even worse incident. He could end up landing face down, or even get some of the shit in his eyes or mouth or ears.

He tries to decide if he's more embarrassed or mad. After a moment, he lands on mad. He cusses and screams like a sailor, but then remembers he's at work. He concentrates on not slipping as he stands. Just as he starts to make some real progress, he falls again. He gets some in his hair this time.

"It's okay, Henry. There are spare hazmat suits in the back of the van."

"Am I gonna fucking die from this? This shit can be toxic, you know." The panic on Henry's face is clear.

"Maybe you should try yoga. In yoga you learn to balance and right yourself in any situation. I do it three times a week," James says. He's genuinely trying to help, but as Henry's face grows a deep purple with rage, I step in.

"You go get the hazmat suit and I'll meet you in the van. I got this."

Henry stands with some help from me and storms off. I check my watch. 2:59 p.m. Okay, this better really be the last call for a while. It's starting to cut close. I need to be in my seat when the puck drops at 5:15 p.m.

On our way to drop off the body, I drop Henry off at home for a shower and change of clothes. He doesn't stop going on and on about the dangers of toxoplasmosis. The more he talks, the less I want to be in the same vehicle with him covered in cat shit.

I make it to the arena, grab a hot dog, and find my seat in time to hear the anthem and see the puck drop. I enjoy the first and second periods undisturbed, but just as the third period starts, I feel the buzz of my phone in my pocket. I close my eyes, take a deep breath, and try not to get mad. Maybe it's Dad letting me know he doesn't need me for the rest of the day. It's him, but it's not such good news.

"Some jogger just spotted a body in a lake. Get down there." The anger is clear in his voice. He doesn't want to be talking to me.

"Can it wait a half hour? If it's in a lake, it's not like there's any need to hurry, right?"

"Get your ass down there! There's no one else to get it. Joel is on the west side at a multiple shooting and Henry is in the emergency room. He swears he caught an infection from your last call."

"Are you kidding?"

Silence on the other end of the line.

"Okay, okay, I'll get there as soon as I can. I'm downtown right now."

"Move your ass, now!"

And with that, he hangs up. Fuck it, I'll wait ten minutes. Clearly he's not going to fire me in any situation. The buzzer sounds and the game heads into overtime. My phone rings again.

"Where are you?"

"I'm on my way, alright?" I say, only half paying attention. The game is getting more exciting by the moment.

"The fuck you are! I just saw you on TV at a fucking hockey game! This is the last time I tell you. *Get there!*"

"What are we, Dominos? Thirty minutes or it's free? It's a floater. I'll be there when I get there!" I shout.

"You'd better be there in five or I'm going to call you non-stop until I hear from the coroner that you're on site."

"What are you gonna do, fire me? Whatever." Now I'm actively trying to get fired. I'm not going to get stuck in this job for the rest of my life. If my dad refuses to let me quit, he can deal with whatever I dish out until he fires me himself.

I leave just as the game ends and get stuck in traffic leaving the arena. By the time I get to the address Dad sent me, it's well over an hour since his first call.

The body is face down and floating in the lake. I use the word lake loosely here. It's more of a bog, the kind filled with mosquitos in the summer and duck shit all year round.

James pulls in a few minutes after me and glances at the water from the parking lot. "Scoop it out of the water, put it in a body bag, and take it to the morgue. Time of death, 8:27 p.m." He doesn't even get out of the car. He rolls up the window and pulls out of the lot, leaving me alone with the police divers. They wade into the disgusting sludge water to retrieve the body. I stand on the bank and watch. There's a horrible smell of decomposition as soon as they move the body. I catch a glimpse of bones and chunks of flesh covered in algae, long chunks of reeds, and other general water funkiness. The divers kick up other things in the water like soggy cigarette packs and used condoms. They get the body in the body bag, zip it up, and put it gently on the bank where I can reach it. I fetch the bag and some of the water gets on me while I'm lifting it onto the gurney. I gag. I put it in the back of the van and head for the morgue. The drive is one of the longest and worst-smelling of my life.

When I get to the morgue, I pull the bag off the gurney and put it on an exam table. I turn back to the empty gurney and realize it's covered in hundreds of maggots. Wiggling, disgusting maggots. I hate maggots so completely that a shudder runs up my back and I start hyperventilating. I check the bag and sure enough, there's a small tear where it must have snagged on something. More maggots wiggle their way out of the bag, and I want to scream. I grab the gurney and turn to leave. There's a trail of maggots and putrid water following my path the entire way in. Great. I bet the van is a mess, too.

Outside in the parking garage under the glare of the garage lights, the back of the van is covered in what looks like one trillion maggots exploring in search of a meal. I want to set the van on fire and walk home. Instead, I head to a car wash. Maybe I can vacuum the little fuckers out.

I manage to get most of them out with a broom and the car wash vacuum. I only feel a little guilty for using a public vacuum. I head home and climb straight into the shower to scrub the day off. I climb into bed, light a joint, turn on the TV, and drift to sleep watching *The Jerk*.

I jolt from a deep sleep after only a few hours. My phone rings but I can't quite place where the sound is coming from. I shake off the sleep enough to grab it, and the moment I answer it, I regret it.

"What the *fuck* did you bring to the morgue!" Dad screams.

"What are you talking about? The floater?"

"Yeah, well, that wasn't a human. It was a dead fucking deer! The whole morgue had to be quarantined because of that bag filled with deer guts and rotten flesh you brought them! The fucking animals are rotten with parasites and disease!"

"How is that my fault? The divers put it in the bag, I take it to the morgue. That's my job. I'm just a driver."

"Well, next time you see James, you'd better apologize to him. The whole department had to be quarantined and cleaned from top to bottom."

"So, I should apologize because no one realized it wasn't a human body? Fuck that. That's not on me. I'm going back to sleep. It's finally my day off and I don't want to think about this anymore."

"If you ever do that stupid shit again, you're gonna be out of a job."

ERIN POTTER-PLOW AND DAVE PLOW

"If I ever do what? My fucking *job*? This is not on me. Shit happens, but you don't blame the delivery driver for the pizza being undercooked. Now fuck off. I'm sleeping." Holy shit, that felt good. I've never talked to him like that, let alone hung up on him. The phone doesn't ring again. I fall asleep in a fog of exhaustion and victorious glee.

CHAPTER TWENTY

"Mr. Plow?"

"Yeah man, Mr. Plow. Like from *The Simpsons*. The one where Homer starts a snowplow business."

Joel takes a long drag from the joint we're sharing and thinks about it. "Yeah, that's a cool name for your solo act. And you're only doing comedy stuff?"

"Pretty much. Maybe some parody stuff. I don't know."

"And you're not quitting The Hairy Areolas?"

"No!"

"Then I think it's rad. Maybe I'll do something solo someday."

I've stressed about this conversation for the past few weeks, but like a bandage getting ripped off, I just sprung it on Joel. I'm relieved he's taking it well. We stand in the driveway outside his house after band practice. Myrna pops her head out the front door.

"Hey Dave! You can't leave until you try one of the Mexican wedding cakes I just made!" She disappears back into the house and the screen door slams behind her.

"Dude, they are so gross, but you can't let her think that her baking is shitty so just pop the whole thing in your mouth and smile and say 'yum'. I'll owe you one."

Myrna bounds out the front door with a plate covered in tiny white balls of pastry. They don't smell half bad. "I thought something a little exotic might be fun for the wedding instead of traditional cake. I've been baking things to try. Last week I did these little Italian custard things, but they didn't really turn out."

Joel proposed to Myrna in a spur of the moment a few weeks ago. Their cat Banana had a seizure on the kitchen floor and she gave him mouth-to-mouth and saved him. He says any woman who would give mouth-to-mouth to a cat is a keeper.

"I'm sure you'll find one that's perfect. Let me try one of these bad boys." I'm stoned, and just as I put one of the powdered-sugar-coated balls in my mouth, I take a deep breath, inhaling the powder and choking instantly.

"Oh god, you hate them!"

"No he doesn't, babe. You don't hate them, right Dave?"

I cough and cough, only able to shake my head. Finally clearing the dust from my throat, there's one flavor overwhelming my mouth. Salt. "It's good Myrna… Salty."

"*Salty*?" Myrna turns on her heel and bolts for the front door.

"What the fuck, man?"

"I'm sorry, that's all I could taste!"

"I know. They're fucking disgusting!"

We both erupt in laughter.

"I gotta go. I have to stop by the office to drop off some paperwork for Henry, and then I have a blind date."

"You have a date?" Joel's mouth hangs open.

"Yeah. My dad has a friend from the country club with a daughter he's convinced I should marry, or some shit."

"I hope she's as good for you as Myrna is for me. You need someone to help you…relax."

"I'll be happy if she doesn't think I'm a weirdo for doing this job."

I pull into the driveway behind the cemetery and park my van next to my dad's. Things are getting better between us, but I still can't resist being a smartass to him every chance I get. The inequality is shifting in our relationship, and I'm determined to make us as close to equals as I can.

I walk into the trailer and hear the end of his conversation with someone on the phone. He glances up and immediately barks, "I'm gonna have to call you back." He slams the phone down.

"I'm just dropping off Henry's paperwork from today. He had to go early. Said something about his mom needing a ride to get her ingrown toenail removed."

Dad mimes vomiting. "Are you ready for tonight? You're not wearing that, are you?"

"What's wrong with this?" I look down at my black Iron Maiden T-shirt sticking out from under my unbuttoned white dress shirt, black slacks with a little dirt on them, and black Vans.

"This girl is a JAP. You'd better up your game if you're gonna impress her."

"Shouldn't she be more worried about impressing me? Also, Jewish American Princess is a slur these days, Dad."

"Whatever. Either way, you'd better shower and put on some nice clothes. Her dad is a very rich, very important defense attorney. You could be living the good life with that kind of family money."

"I don't care about money. I like people for who they are."

He snorts and laughs. "Well if it weren't for that family money, she would still have her original nose, and that would have made for a very uncomfortable date for you tonight."

"Jesus, Dad, what the fuck? Why do you always have to say shit like that?"

"Like what, the truth? She was born ugly and turned into a swan." He emphatically bends his finger in air quotes.

"As long as she supports my music career, she has a chance with me."

"Music career?"

"Yeah, I'm a solo act now. Mr. Plow."

"Are you serious?"

"Dead serious, actually."

He laughs again, right to my face. I need to leave before I really lose my temper. I just need to stay on long enough to fund my album, then I am fucking out of here.

CHAPTER TWENTY-ONE

"So Jennifer, what do you do for work?"

We've sat in silence at our table for three horribly uncomfortable minutes.

"I'm going to law school right now, so I intern at my dad's firm. What about you? You work for your dad too, right?" She's pretty, with blonde hair hanging stick-straight down to her chin. She has giant green eyes with a large space between them, making her look more like a baby horse than a woman. She seems to have perfectly flawless skin, but I suspect she's wearing a pound of makeup. Her green silk blouse has a high collar with a giant bow. She looks like she belongs on TV. She starts clicking her long, fake red nails on the table, waiting for me to answer.

"Yeah, I'm a body removal technician. My dad is the director at a funeral home on the east side, at the Jewish cemetery."

"Wait, I thought you were a funeral director too?"

"No, I just pick up the bodies."

"Oh… So what's that like?"

I hate this question. I know that people don't really want to know, so I throw out my standard answer. "It's okay."

"So, are you in school to become a funeral director?"

"No. I actually want to be a musician. I don't really see a career for myself in the funeral industry."

More silence settles over us. The server brings us each a beer.

"Um, I ordered a white zin. I don't want this." She doesn't even let the waiter respond before sending him away with the dismissive wave of a queen to a servant. I've never seen anyone do this in real life. I'm stunned.

"So, what kind of music do you play?"

"Mostly folk, punk, comedy stuff. Like Frank Zappa or acoustic Weird Al."

"Hmm. Okay. I don't really like music. I don't see the appeal."

Jesus, who the fuck doesn't like music? I guess someone who would wave away a server like a stray dog.

"So, do you like, touch the bodies?"

"Yes, that's usually how you get them onto the stretcher."

"Does it, like…excite you?"

"What?"

"You know, sexually?"

I study her face and can't figure out if she's being serious or not. No one has ever asked me that and been serious.

"No. That's disgusting."

"Well I don't know, why the hell else would you do a job like that and not even use it as a stepping-stone to a better career?"

"There actually isn't anyone I work with that would get off sexually from touching a dead person. That's a stereotype. We like to think of ourselves as helpers, more than anything. And we respect the dead."

"Well how would I know? You haven't really told me anything about the job."

Fuck, is this what it's like to date a lawyer? Being interrogated and having your words twisted? I can just imagine if we dated and she knew that I had two female roommates. She'd probably be jealous, demanding I move out just to prove I'm not cheating on her.

The server returns with her wine. "Are you ready to order?" he asks, looking at me.

"I want the Cesar salad to start, but I'm vegan so oil and vinegar dressing on the side. Then I want the eggplant parmigiana for the main course, but don't use an egg wash to keep the breadcrumbs on the eggplant, use coconut milk," she barks at the poor server.

"I'm sorry ma'am, the eggplant parmigiana is prepared off site. We just bake it."

Jennifer rolls her eyes and makes the most god-awful groan. I hate that I'm sitting here with her. She seems like a person who kicks puppies or makes coats from their furs.

"Fine. Just the salad."

He turns to me.

"I'll have the cheeseburger with sweet potato fries. And can you add a fried egg to the burger?"

"But...I'm vegan!"

The server and I stare at her in silence.

"I'm not ordering this for you, I'm ordering it for me." I glance at the server, confused.

"But you can't eat that in front of me! I won't watch you eat something that used to have a face!"

"Well, you don't have to stay and watch."

The server stifles a chuckle.

"If that's what you insist on ordering, I will go. Just for the record, this date did *not* go well." She stands, grabs her purse, and storms out. The server and I both laugh.

"I think you just dodged a bullet," he says.

"I think you're right. I'll take another beer when you get a chance, please."

"On me, man. That was brutal to watch."

97

Is this what it's like to date in the corporate, adult world? Is everyone so obsessed with status and career and titles? Paige seems pretty down to earth. Maybe I just need to date someone within my industry. Or better, in the music industry. Clearly not everyone is going to be as accepting of my job as I hoped.

I sit alone at the fancy table and enjoy the most delicious twenty-five-dollar cheeseburger I've ever had. My head swirls with thoughts of Paige. Her smile, her hair, her perfume. I make a promise to myself then and there that I'll give it a real try with her. I wonder if she would give mouth-to-mouth to a cat to save its life? She probably would.

CHAPTER TWENTY-TWO

There are telltale signs of causes of death that you begin to recognize after some time on the job. When you see a river of shit and blood on the floor, sprayed up the walls and all over the furniture, you know you're there for a GI bleed. One of the worst ways to die.

It's Friday night and Henry and I are called to a townhouse downtown. I'm already annoyed at spending all day with Henry, listening to him describe in painful detail how he's learning to count cards so he can win big at the casino and retire early. I've done all I can to change the subject, but he just keeps pivoting back to goddamn card counting.

We park outside and pull out the stretcher. As I get closer to the door, the smell slaps me in the face. Shit. Not the usual decomp mixed with rot and filth, but actual feces. Sour and pungent on the wind, it eclipses all other smells in the air. A GI bleed for sure. I step inside the front door and see it. A river of brown. When it happens, people seem to totally freak out, usually running from room to room in a panic, trying to figure out what's going on. Why are they pooping themselves uncontrollably? Why won't it stop? Is it even worth trying to make it to the bathroom? The hallmark of a GI bleed is that the person poops themselves to death. I go back to the van for my rubber boots.

There are people all over the house. Investigators, paramedics, and firefighters. A paramedic is puking violently on the sidewalk. Those guys see everything. Seeing a paramedic empty his stomach outside a scene is never a good sign.

Do I search upstairs or down first? Since no one is willing to acknowledge that I'm there or give me information on where the body is, I decide to search for myself. I stand on the landing of the nineteen-sixties split-level house and decide to take my chances with downstairs. I grab the black wrought iron railing and head toward the den. The carpet squishes underneath my boots. I follow the river of brown into the den, back to the hallway, into the laundry room, and out to the adjoining garage. Nothing. I head upstairs, into the living room, past the dining room, and into the hall. The bathroom is clear and so are the bedrooms. Where the hell is the body? That leaves only one room that I breezed past earlier: the kitchen. I come around the corner and there she sits.

The dead woman is collapsed in a heap in the kitchen. She died next to the cabinet labeled "cat food". She's wearing a beautiful green dress, house slippers, and a warm cable-knit gray sweater draped over her tiny frame. She's so small and meek in a pile on the floor. How did this tiny mouse of a woman cover her home in blood and diarrhea? Like, gallons of it? How could her body hold so much liquid? There's even some splattered on the ceiling, which I don't notice until a paramedic points it out to a cop. How the fuck did it get on the ceiling?

She looks like the type of woman who doesn't even take off her bra or stockings until it's time to put on her nightgown. Someone from a more formal generation, like my Nana. It's a shame she ended up covered in her own poop, dying in such an undignified way. She's a relic of a more refined time. A time when women cooked meat in a savory Jell-O and called it aspic. When you used a pickle fork, and hand-washed your stockings before lovingly hanging them to dry on the shower rod.

Henry is silent while we're in the home. Mostly. Thank goodness for small blessings. I just want two minutes of fucking silence from his non-stop yammering. It's getting harder and harder to keep up this schedule of being on call twenty-four hours a day. I'm beyond exhausted, and lately I'm starting to think that a human being could actually die from sleep deprivation. Paige confirms my fears once we got to the hospital morgue.

"You can totally die from being sleep deprived," she tells me cheerfully as she takes the paperwork for the dead woman.

"How does that even work? I fall asleep and never wake up again?"

"Well, no. Not like that. But you can be so tired that you don't realize you're drinking bleach instead of your morning energy drink, or accidentally leave the gas turned on but forget to light the pilot light. Stuff like that. Why?"

"Oh, you know, just feel like I'm slipping further and further into madness with this job. Being on call, never getting more than an hour or so of sleep in a row on the days I work."

"That's not good. You need to make sure you're taking care of yourself." Paige stands next to me while she finishes signing my drop-off paperwork. Her hair smells like strawberries. I suddenly want to grab her and hug her and bury my face in her hair so I can inhale every bit of strawberry essence on her. I want to get rid of this fucking smell of death stuck in my nose and keep her smell with me all day.

"Seriously, are you okay? You look kind of…exhausted." She looks me up and down.

"Yeah, I'm okay. I'll go home and relax after this." As if that's even remotely possible, working for my dad. He recently offered me a "raise" where I work only four days a week but get paid the same salary as working five days a week. I took it, of course, because I'm desperate for a chance to get some more sleep and still be able to record my album. I have twenty-two songs ready to record. "Hey Paige? Would you wanna, I don't know…have dinner with me sometime?"

101

What the hell just came out of my mouth?

"Hmm…" She sticks the tip of her pen in her mouth while she ponders the question.

"I mean, no pressure or anything. Just, like, a burger. Or not. Whatever."

"Sure! How about next week? I have to go out of town, but I'll be back the nineteenth." She smiles at me and I smile back. She has a big black dot on her lip from the ink in the tip of her pen. Oh well. At least she's not a vegan. I think. I fucking hope not.

My phone rings, startling me. I jump a little and immediately feel stupid. "Gotta take this. See ya then!" I head for the door as I answer my phone, trying not to look stupid as I leave.

CHAPTER TWENTY-THREE

Jumpers are awful. Mostly because depending on what they jump off of, they either splat or smear. Today is a splat. Along the edge of the inlet where the water flows in from the ocean, there's nothing but jagged rocks and boulders that slope down into the water. More of the same awaits anyone that ventures into the water.

When someone decides to jump off a bridge, the last thing they think about is the mechanics of the act itself. When this woman jumped, she didn't take into account the trajectory she would need to land in the deep water and not on the jagged rocks that would definitely create a splat. She was probably only thinking how she'd finally gotten up the courage to jump.

I have the luxury of not having to go out on the water to retrieve the body. The Coast Guard is in charge of that part. Henry and I wait on the shore. He's bitching about the latest in the continuing drama with his landlord. He lives in a tiny basement suite, AKA the half-finished basement of a Greek woman who charges him way too much rent and cooks the same thing for every meal. Though it's indistinguishable what that one meal actually is, Henry is one hundred percent convinced that it's just a giant bulb of garlic, by itself.

"That lady must just have garlic oozing out of her pores. No wonder all she has is her weird, half-dead dog and no husband. That bitch stinks! And she's shitty at recycling. I'm always having to re-sort the stuff she tosses in the bins," Henry gripes.

I love Henry's weird obsession with recycling, and right now it's helping me forget how annoyed I've been with him today. Blatant disregard for the process of recycling always gets him worked into a frenzy. Of course, he sees nothing wrong with stealing the neighbor's Wi-Fi or stealing cans from sleeping homeless campers so he can cash them in to get money for smokes. I guess morality is only half his strong suit.

As the Coast Guard boat approaches, we get our stretcher ready. She hasn't been in the water long, so she won't have that additional stink of inlet water. That's a silver lining. The Coast Guardsmen laugh and joke as they climb off the boat.

"I bet the fish are having one great meal tonight!"

"Yeah, it was nice that her final act was to give back to the circle of life."

Great. These assholes are going to make some tasteless joke and expect me to laugh.

"Hey man, check it out," says the first guy. "This lady's boob is missing!"

The sailors stand around making boob jokes. I wait for them to finish so they can release the body to me. Henry joins in and I tune them out completely. I daydream about that sad, single breast being eaten by fish. I wish that boob at least had a happier end to its story than the woman it came from. I imagine it hitchhiking to Alaska to live off the land, making friends and having adventures along the way. Sharing its dreams with other travelers riding the rails. Learning how to catch a fish and cook it over a makeshift fire, or how to hunt for edible berries. Staring up at the night sky, counting the stars and feeling a sense of wonder at how big the universe is and how small that one little boob is. And then a few weeks into winter the boob would realize it needed more adequate shelter to make it through the long dead of winter and the unavoidable cold of the Alaskan wilderness. It might panic and try to make its way back to the city, only to be eaten by a bear who mistook it for a salmon.

As I stand daydreaming about a cartoon breast with a little stick over its shoulder and a bandana filled with snacks, I realize I'm standing there like an asshole with a smile on my sleep-deprived face while everyone stares at me.

"Dave, what are you doing? Are you okay?"

"I'm fine, why? Why is everyone fucking looking at me?"

"Because you just shouted out 'The littlest hobo! But it's a boob!' and then you started singing that Cat Stevens song about the father and son," Henry says cautiously.

"No, I didn't."

"You totally just did. You don't remember? It literally just happened." Henry stares at me, his mouth hanging open.

"Fuck off! All of you." I'm startled and worried at the same time because I really don't remember doing it. It's possible, I guess, since everyone is looking at me like I'm insane. "Let's just get this call done."

"Don't go too far, boys. There's another body on the north side of the shore. Make room for a second in there and I'll see you on the other side of the bay," says the Coast Guard commander.

Shit! I want to go the fuck home!

Henry and I drive around to the north side.

"Are you okay, dude?" He's so genuinely concerned that I feel guilty for being such a dick to him earlier.

"I'm just so goddamn tired all the time. It's like I never feel rested, even when I sleep a full eight hours. I don't know what to do anymore."

"You need a vacation, man. Or maybe a new job. Or both."

"Yeah, I really do."

We finish fetching the second body from the Coast Guard and head to the hospital to drop them off at the morgue. Henry drives because I don't trust myself right now.

"I hear you have a hot date coming up, Dave."

"Who told you that?"

"Joel. He said you finally got the balls to ask out that hot coroner. You'd better get some sleep before that date. You want to make sure your dick works before you take a woman like that out."

I'm so tired it feels like I'm outside my body, watching someone else have this conversation. "Don't talk about her like that, Henry. She's a nice person."

"She can be nice and nasty at the same time," Henry cackles.

"Well, all that matters to me is if she can give a cat mouth-to-mouth. I'll marry that girl if she can give a cat CPR. That's how you know she's a good one."

"Whatever you say, you crazy, sleepy bastard."

CHAPTER TWENTY-FOUR

Wednesday is my favorite day of the work week. The morgue downtown always has doughnuts and coffee. I don't know if it's because everyone needs a little extra motivation to power through until Friday, or maybe because Tuesday nights are bowling league for the morgue. Either way, the medical examiners are always hung over and ready for some fresh coffee and greasy doughnuts.

James has a whiteboard in the main office where he writes interesting facts related to death. The weirder, the better. He always says that the point of the whiteboard is to teach and broaden the minds of everyone who comes to the morgue.

"How weird does a case have to be to make your Case of the Week board?" I ask him between sips of scalding coffee.

"The weirder, the better. Weirder than my Google alerts for the week."

"One of these days I'm gonna bring you one that makes it on that board. If it's a good one, you owe me a joint and a steak dinner."

"You got it," James laughs.

Two days later, I get my weird case.

A dead woman in her late sixties is found her in her kitchen, face down with her hand in the cat food dish.

Joel and I walk the gurney into the home and find everyone milling around. I'm about to ask someone what's going on, when I hear it. It sounds like an alarm, the kind on an old dryer, a strange, muffled buzzing noise.

Everyone in ear shot is searching for the source of the sound.

"What is that?" Joel asks.

"That is precisely what we're trying to figure out," says a cop.

Joel scrunches his eyes closed. He looks like a confused pug listening for the garbage truck. He clamps a hand over one ear and cranes his neck in the direction of the refrigerator. He tries in vain to heighten the hearing in the one ear so as to narrow down the possible source.

I almost instantly recognize what the noise is. The unmistakable sound of a cheap, battery-operated device. I recognize it because of a summer temp job I had a few years back in an adult warehouse. They all sound the same. It's also obviously coming from inside the dead woman. "It's a vibrator," I say.

"No... No, that can't be right," says Joel. He sits with what I've said for a few seconds before he points down at her body with a look of disbelief and horror as he realizes I'm right. For a moment all semblance of professionalism is abandoned as a round of disgusted noises, groans, and a single profanity fill the room.

The dead woman wears a pair of house slippers and a cotton night gown. The detective reaches out slowly with the tip of his shoe and gently nudges her body. The buzzing stops for just a moment and then resumes.

When James finally gets to the scene to investigate the cause of death, I'm giddy. I can almost guarantee this one is whiteboard worthy. "I think this is it. This is the one that makes Case of the Week," I say to James as he bends down to check for a pulse.

"Oh yeah, why is that?"

"Because I'll give you one guess what that noise is."

Joel and I choke down meatloaf sandwiches, the daily special at Lucille's downtown. My phone rings and it's my dad with another call, this one forty-five minutes from where we're eating.

An hour later we pulled up to the curb in front of a home and find the cops waiting for us. We're greeted with silence as we approach the front door with the stretcher.

"He's in the bathroom, in the bathtub. He's been there for about a week. Good luck with that," the grouchy cop says as we start past him toward the bathroom.

As soon as we set foot in the bathroom it's clear that this is going to be a huge pain in the ass. The bathroom is tiny. The toilet is wedged between the tub and a pedestal sink, all crammed into a room not much bigger than a small closet.

The guy is well over six feet tall. What's left of his feet hang over the edge of the tub, surrounded by putrid water.

"Towel trick?" Joel asks.

I nod. The towel trick also works with sheets—any kind of fabric, really. You take one towel for each limb and place the towel underneath. Then, twist the towel like a tourniquet until it's as tight as possible around the ankle or wrist joint, and use that to lift the person out of the tub. That way, instead of grabbing a limb and having the skin and muscle slide off in your hand, you get a solid grip on them and get them out of the tub and onto the stretcher in one movement.

Joel and I each take two towels and get to work twisting. I climb on top of the toilet to get a better grip on the arms. What should happen is we easily hoist the body out of the tub of fluids, decay, and insects into the waiting body bag on the stretcher. This is not what happens.

Our 'heaving' is out of sync. Unprepared, I drop the arms at the same moment Joel lifts the bottom half of the man out of the tub. The bottom half of the man drapes over the side while the upper half submerges completely in the black, stagnant water.

I stand teetering on top of the toilet, one hand on the top of the door, the other trying in vain to grasp the tile wall. Joel decides he's going to try and leverage the legs into the bag anyways, pulling the rest of the body out of the water on his own. The waterlogged body is heavier than it looks and Joel only succeeds in getting about three more inches out of the tub, sloshing human soup all over himself in the process.

Like a kitten being splashed with water for the first time, Joel shrieks loudly and drops the legs, trying frantically to wipe the slime from his face. With his eyes tightly clamped shut, he feels around for something to wipe his face with. His weight shifts in such a way that he immediately loses his footing and falls. His hands extend in front of him, directly onto the sopping wet floor and into even more of the sludge that's now sloshing over the side of the tub. He whimpers pathetically.

I stand perched above the putrid scene, not moving a muscle lest Joel drag me into the human soup with him. He finally stops thrashing, surrendering to the fact that it's too late and there's no saving himself. He slowly opens his eyes to survey the damage and sees me completely unsullied and hovering above the horror.

"Please tell me there's something I can change into in the van."

"There's a hazmat suit left over from who knows how long ago. Do you want me to get that for you?"

"No. I'll change outside."

Part of me feels horrible, looking into the eyes of my best friend as he's covered in the worst things imaginable. I can't believe I did this to him. I know he begged for the job, but how could he have truly known what he was asking for?

The other part of me wants to laugh because it really is the funniest thing I've seen in a long time, watching him Mr. Bean his way around the bathroom, slipping and sliding. If he wasn't so pissed it would have been the perfect bonding moment. A story to tell our buddies. A shared misery. I can't believe my dad wants this life for me. Aren't our parents supposed to want better for us than they had?

Joel exits the room and I'm left standing atop a dead man's toilet until fifteen minutes later when he returns in a hazmat suit with clearly nothing on underneath. I can't say I blame him, but those suits are not built for modesty and I see more of Joel than I ever want to. I avoid making eye contact while we salvage the situation and load the dead man into the propped open body bag.

"I feel shitty. I know you wanted this job, but I'm sure you didn't think it would be like this."

"Are you crazy? I mean yeah, this is a gross job, but it's also exciting and weird and important."

"You don't hate it? Or me, for getting you into it?"

"No! If I hated it, I would have quit a long time ago. I mean, come on. This isn't a job that gets better over time. You have no reason to feel bad."

CHAPTER TWENTY-FIVE

"This is Doug Emerson from Revenue Canada. I need to speak with David."

I just answered my phone with my eyes still closed, not expecting to hear an unfamiliar voice. I was in a deep sleep, dreaming about being on stage playing for a crowd in an arena. I was naked except for a pair of brown socks, and for some reason the only song I knew how to play was "Do-Wacka-Do". Everyone hated it and threw their beers at the stage.

"This is David."

"I need you to come to our offices. I have some questions about your payroll."

"I don't have anything to do with payroll. I'm an employee, not an owner."

"We need you to come in today at 10:30 a.m. Come to the downtown offices, suite 160." With that, the line went dead.

What the fuck was that about? I glance at the clock. It's 9:15 a.m. I slowly rub the sleep out of my eyes and remember it's supposed to be my day off. The last thing I want to do is spend my day off at Revenue Canada.

I hop in the shower, throw on a clean D.O.A. T-shirt, a black pair of Dickies pants, my Vans, and a black baseball hat worn backwards. I drink two cups of black coffee, smoke three cigarettes, and call it breakfast.

I arrive at the offices and make my way to suite 160. Behind a reception desk is the most unfriendly person the department could have possibly hired. A Bea Arthur look-alike with a chilly demeanor to match.

"I'm here for a 10:30 meeting."

"With whom are you meeting?"

"Doug, I think."

"You think, or you know?"

"Doug is who called me this morning, so I'm assuming it's with him."

She rolls her eyes and lets out an annoyed moan. Flipping through the papers on her desk, she asks my name and I tell her.

"Oh… Okay, I see. Down the hall, second door on the left. Doug is waiting for you."

"Okay, thanks. Should I be worried? What is this about?"

"Yes, you should be. Now if I were you, I'd get in there and not waste any more time."

Great. I make my way down the hall to the door. Am I supposed to knock? Do I just walk in? The last thing I want to do is piss off a revenue agent. They can be a huge pain in the ass.

"Are you going to stand there all day or are you going to go in?" she barks at me from the front office.

"Do I knock first? Or just…?"

"Knock."

I knock three times and wait. The door opens and inside is a man who looks at me like I kicked his mother and called her a whore. He stands a solid five foot four at most with a mop of curly hair on top of his head, kept longish and combed straight up to add a few extra inches to his height. He wears a dark blue suit and a pair of tiny round glasses.

"Come in, David. I'm Doug. Do you know why I called you down here today?" He sits down behind a large desk that makes him look like a miniature figure in an oversized dollhouse.

Cutting straight to the chase. Not a good sign. "No, not really."

"Well, over the last twenty-four hours I've audited your payroll taxes from the past few years. We have a real problem."

"What's that?"

"You've been working at Funeral Services Unlimited for the past three years, but you have never once paid your taxes. Care to explain?"

"Wait, what do you mean?"

"I mean that you have not paid your taxes. That's illegal."

"I know it is. That's why payroll deducts it from my paycheck every two weeks. They take it out and pay it. Since when is an employee supposed to be in charge of paying their own taxes? I mean, I file the annual ones like everyone else."

"Yes, you file your annual income taxes, but I'm talking about payroll taxes. The quarterly ones. I don't know what your arrangement is with your employer, but we've never received a tax payment from you as long as you've worked there."

"Every two weeks my dad gives us—all his employees—handwritten personal checks. I just assumed he was giving us the amount after payroll taxes."

Doug turns and types at his computer. He sits reading and scrolling down the screen. "Who is this? You both have the same last name and he's listed as CEO." He turns his screen toward me and points to a name.

"That's my dad."

"That's your dad?"

"Yeah, why?"

"Are you sure that the taxes are taken out of your paycheck?"

"I don't get a paystub, it's just a handwritten check. I guess I just assumed that the taxes were being taken out."

"Think carefully, because what you're implying is that your father, the CEO of the company, is taking the taxes out of your checks but not paying the government. That's embezzling, and it's a very serious charge."

"He's my dad. He wouldn't do that to me. To any of us. Have you talked to anyone else from the company?"

"I have meetings today with Joel, Henry, and Kyle. You're listed as CFO, so we called you in first."

"CFO? I'm not the CFO. There is no CFO. It's just my dad, and he's paid the same guy to be his accountant since I was a little kid."

"What's his name?"

I give him the name of our longtime family accountant and he types in the info.

"We'll be looking into this for as long as it takes to figure out, so don't go leaving the city or anything. After I talk with your coworkers and father, I'll be in touch."

"Wait. If you're talking to them too, that must mean they haven't paid their taxes either. Are you saying he's been taking money from *all* of us?"

"I'm not saying anything. I legally can't comment on it. You're free to go now."

It all hits me at once. How long have they been looking into this? How did they notice? How can they hold me responsible? Who the fuck listed me as CFO on paperwork I've never seen? What the fuck is going on?

CHAPTER TWENTY-SIX

I can't control my anger. I leave Revenue Canada and drive straight to the office. I storm in and slam the door behind me. My dad sits in his chair eating an ice cream sandwich.

"What the fuck is going on?"

We stare at each other for a moment before he smiles, oblivious to my mood. "I'm having a snack, and then I have to figure out what to do with that old guy we left in a drawer at the morgue downtown. They called today saying they need the space, and we have to come get him."

"Wait, what! You never went back to get that guy? The same guy you left sitting in the parking garage for weeks?"

"Yeah, same one. What's got your skirt all bunched up?"

I shake with anger while he sits there slurping melted ice cream off his fingers. "Well, let's start with the meeting I just had at Revenue Canada, then we can move on to when I was appointed CFO. Then we can talk about where the fuck all the money is that you kept out of our paychecks that's supposed to be going to payroll taxes. It had to go somewhere, and it sure as fuck didn't go to me."

His face is shocked for just a moment, then he quickly regains his composure. "What did you say to Revenue Canada?"

"The fucking truth! That I don't know what they're talking about and that I didn't embezzle any money."

"Hmm. Okay. Smart move."

"Smart move? It's the truth! Where's the money?"

"I don't know what you're talking about."

"Okay, fine. When did I become the CFO of this company?"

"It's just a title I put down on some papers so that if anything happens to me, you get the business."

"I don't want the business! Now it looks like I'm some kind of co-conspirator!"

"Don't be so dramatic."

"How can you be so…so…un-fucking-worried about all this!"

"I'm worried about one thing, and that's finding a place for the man at the morgue who's getting evicted."

"That's your problem, and so is this. You'd better fix it! You can't make me take the fall for you!"

"No one is falling. Just calm down, Davey Boy."

"Don't you fucking call me that!" I slam my hands down on his desk. Steam is ready to actually come out of my ears. I imagine grabbing him by his sloping, old man shoulders and shaking him until he starts to behave like he gives a fuck. We stare at each other in silence. "Well, I guess let's just say fuck it, right? Since you don't seem to understand or care what a big deal this is, fuck it, why should I?"

He looks surprised. "Exactly. When I worry, that's when you can worry."

"This is exhausting. It's like I'm trying to explain to a caveman what germs are." I shake my head and go to the door. I feel like a crazy person, talking to him.

"Oh, come on. Don't get your panties twisted. It's not a big deal. Now, what is a big deal is I heard that you asked the shiksa coroner out on a date. Not a good idea. I think—"

I storm out and slam the door, shaking the trailer. "*Fuuuuck!*" I scream at the top of my lungs, frustration seeping from my every pore. Am I crazy? Why am I the only one worried about this? What else is going on with this business that I don't know about? I sit in the driveway as I've done so many times before and think about what to do next. I light a smoke and turn on the radio, but I can't concentrate on the music. I can't slow down my thoughts. I can't even see straight. My arms tingle again and panic eclipses my every thought and feeling. I want to scream. I feel like I'm dying. This keeps happening, and I haven't even bothered to address it yet. I keep thinking I'll feel better when I get some sleep, or that it'll be better tomorrow, but it never is. It's getting worse.

I turn off my phone and roll down the windows, throwing it in reverse. I have more important things going on today than this bullshit. I have a date to get ready for.

CHAPTER TWENTY-SEVEN

"That's totally fucked up!"

"I know. It's crazy, right?"

Paige and I are at a steak restaurant for our date, sitting at a candlelit table in a corner of the dark restaurant. We're two drinks in when I tell her about my Revenue Canada meeting.

"He didn't even act like he knew what you were talking about?"

"Nope. Didn't seem even a bit concerned."

Her dark curls are wild tonight. She's wearing a tight black T-shirt and skintight black jeans. Her eyes twinkle when she smiles, and her smell is intoxicating. How can one woman have so many different smells? Tonight she smells like vanilla and cinnamon. She's unbelievably beautiful.

"Do people ever ask you stupid questions because of the field we're in?"

"Like, do we get sexually aroused by the dead bodies?"

"So you've heard that one before, too."

"Yep. My girlfriends always want to know about the penises. Or if I keep a record of the sizes of all the dicks I see," she laughs.

"Did someone really ask you that?"

"Yeah, a guy I went on a date with a few weeks ago. I told him I didn't think about dicks like that, especially on dead men. You should have seen his face!" She takes a large drink of her beer and flips her curls back carelessly. It is the sexiest thing I have ever seen. She's so easy to talk to, and seems to have absolutely no idea how gorgeous she is.

"Or how people use us to gauge how normal their life is. Like, 'I thought my job was weird and then I met you'. That kind of bullshit."

"Try being the only female coroner in the lower mainland! Thank goodness there are three of us now, but for a while there I was the only one."

"My roommates always bitch that my clothes reek of chemicals and dead people."

"Tell me about it! I've tried everything. Dry cleaning, laundry service, bleach...everything!" she says.

Did I just solve the mystery of the many perfumes?

The server brings us our burgers and two more beers.

"Oh my *gawd,* this smells amazing! Smell this!" She shoves her burger at me.

"I have the same burger! I know how good it smells."

"Oh yeah. D'oh!"

We laugh. We haven't stopped laughing since we sat down.

"Are you a *Simpsons* fan?" I ask.

"I love The Simpsons!"

"I just started this new solo acoustic music act. My stage name is Mr. Plow. I do comedy punk songs."

"Like Kevin Bloody Wilson?"

"Yes! No one has ever heard of him! How do you know about him?"

"My dad loved him. I would love to come to one of your shows."

"Okay, I'll let you know when. Joel and I also play in a band. It's more punk stuff, but we have a show next week, if you want to come."

"Cool! I honestly like heavy metal more than punk, but punk is alright. I had no idea you were so into music."

How did I think this woman was annoying? How did I misjudge her so badly? We talk about music, TV shows, records, and comedians for almost three hours. We finally exit the restaurant and stand on the street talking about comic books and movies.

"Well, this has been fun, but I have to work tomorrow. You do too, I'm sure," she says.

"Yeah, I do. This was fun."

Neither of us move. The traffic noise echoes around us, but it feels like the entire city has stopped. We're the only two people in the whole world.

"Well, see ya soon!" Paige throws her arms around me and plants a tiny kiss on my cheek. Before I know it, she's bounding off toward her car on the other side of the street. Her long legs wobble like a baby giraffe as she crosses and when she gets to her car, she turns and waves. Then she hops in her car and is gone.

I walk on air the entire way home. It's like my day started when I saw her face. I can imagine getting used to this feeling. Maybe this is what I've been missing these last few years. Someone to be with. Some love and light. Someone to come home to after a long, shitty day and hug. I miss the simple act of being close to someone who's warm and alive and smells like something magical every time I get near her.

CHAPTER TWENTY-EIGHT

The call comes in and once again I don't want to get out of bed. Even though it's well past 8 a.m., it's still dark out. Every part of me wants to pull the sheets over my head and go back to sleep. My joints ache, which I guess is going to be a thing now, thanks to this job. My shoulders, my knees, and especially my back never stop hurting. Lifting dead weight is degrading my body as much as the nature of the job is degrading my state of mind.

On the days I work, I never seem to get more than an hour or two of sleep at a time. On my days off I'm supposed to do all the things that other people do on their days off, except I'm exhausted. I sleep for the entire first day, then try desperately to enjoy the remaining time I have before my week starts all over again. It feels like more and more people are dying each week, just to fuck with me. Just to make sure I never, ever sleep. The only good thing that's happened was my night with Paige. I've been riding that high for a few days now.

I drag myself out of bed, take a handful of Tylenol with codeine for the pains in my body, and head out the door in search of a fresh pack of smokes and the biggest coffee I can find. I meet Joel at our usual spot, the 7-Eleven at the corner of Main and Chester. Joel has a long black leather duster that he wears during the fall that makes him stand out like a sore thumb in the crowd of morning commuters. This morning he has on a giant black hat with a wide brim. It looks like you could fill the middle with guacamole and line the brim with chips to match the stupid coat. He hops in the van and before

I can say a word, he grins at me.

"Look what I got at the Salvation Army last night! Sweet, right?"

"Dude, it's an old church lady's funeral hat." I barely contain my laughter.

"Fuck you. You're just jealous I found it first. You fucking wish you looked this good in a hat, motherfucker."

"I'm sorry, I'm sorry. It's cool. You look like The Undertaker from WWE—if he got his hats from a lost and found box at the local free clinic."

"All I hear are the jealous words of a loser who doesn't have my confidence to rock this hat."

Touché.

Joel and I pull up to the house of our first call. Everything immediately feels off. We hop out and make our way up the front steps, which upon closer inspection are just crumbling stumps of concrete.

"Hey, guys," says the detective as we approach the door. "What we have here is an elderly brother and sister. The sister was caregiver for the brother. It looks like she died first. She's been in the living room in a lounge chair for at least a week, maybe ten days. The brother was bedridden, and it looks like he tried to get out of bed when he realized something was wrong. That's when he fell and broke his hip, or leg, or something. He tried to drag himself into the main part of the house to call for help but never made it. Now, we're still processing the house, so be careful."

"We're always careful, man," Joel snaps.

"No, I mean because the house is crumbling. There's piles of rat shit, old garbage, moth balls, and tons of cash."

"Cash?"

"Yes, thousands of dollars of it. We're still trying to count and catalog it. If you see a stack we haven't gotten to, let us know."

"Okay," Joel says.

It stinks inside. To be expected, I guess. The smell is a mixture of filth and the sting of rat shit. The dust is so thick that as we walk it swirls in small clouds around our feet. I imagine a tiny dust devil making its way down the long dark hallway, sweeping away any sense of time or urgency with it. The place is dingy and drab and frozen in time. There are newspapers piled everywhere. And rats. So many rats.

We start with the sister. She's in the front of the house and easiest to get to. She's so small and frail, it takes no effort at all to lift her. Then we move on to the brother, who's on the floor in the bedroom. The only problem is we don't know which bedroom. I open the first door in the hall and find a small office. The police have probably already processed this room. There are no stacks of money in sight and the crime scene technicians have left clusters of little yellow plastic cones marking evidence. I close the door and continue on. Behind door number two is a bathroom. A cop sits on a tiny wooden stool counting money. He sits between a pink bathtub with a ring of filth around it the color of melted chocolate and a pink toilet that's clogged with what I also choose to believe is melted chocolate.

"Who lives like this? I had to use the Vicks VapoRub just to stand being in here!" he says to his partner as we pass. You can always tell who's going to be useless at a scene. Anytime you see a thick dollop of ointment on someone's upper lip and shoved up their nostrils, you know.

Door number three is the right one. There, face down on the floor, is the brother. He's wearing black silk pajamas that are clean despite the surrounding filth. We lift his frail body onto the stretcher, and as I bend down to grab his feet, I come face to face with a fat rat. Behind the rat, under the bed, is a giant stack of money.

"I'll finish up here, Joel, and meet you outside in a few."

"Want to go to Bob's Sub for lunch?" he asks as he backs down the hallway.

"Yeah, that sounds good. I'll be right there." I kneel down and grab the stack of money. There are bundles of hundred-dollar bills. Ten neatly-stacked bundles of hundreds.

No one would ever know. I could stick the money in my underwear, socks, or pockets and no one would be able to tell. I could walk out the door, get in the car, and drive away. I could go to this year's WrestleMania. I could buy a new car and finally stop pumping money into my fifteen-year-old van that's always in need of repair. I could take Paige to L.A. I could go to Vegas, New York...*anywhere*, and finally have a real vacation. Away from all the bodies, the death, the calls in the middle of the night to pick someone up who choked on a chicken bone, died on the toilet, or jumped in front of a bus. I could sleep and relax and forget about all the death.

There's no way I can walk out and have no one notice, is there? Somebody will stop me, search me, ask questions. Won't they? What if the brother haunts me for stealing his money? Maybe he'll short out the electrical circuits on my TV and fry it, or rearrange the chairs in my dining room like in *Poltergeist*. What if he opens and slams my cupboard doors all night long until I go insane, or pulls all the doors off the hinges? I would lose the security deposit on my place, for sure.

Or, what if it's cursed blood money? Like Nazi money? If I bought a new car with cursed Nazi money it would definitely crash, and maybe not even kill me. It would just leave me a paralyzed vegetable. What if I started not being able to sleep without seeing the dead man in my nightmares as a rotting corpse? And what if then I got sick and my dick turned black and fell off, and even with all the money I stole I couldn't buy myself a new dick that worked just as good as the original one? Not worth it. Not even a little bit. I get up and walk out, not a single bill taken.

"There's a stack of money under the brother's bed."

"Did you help yourself to a little before you told me?" the cop asks jokingly.

"Nah. I don't want my dick to turn black and fall off."

CHAPTER TWENTY-NINE

I call my dad at the end of my rope to tell him I'm going home, and that if any more calls come in, he can find someone else. I'm exhausted, I'm seeing double, and there's no way I should be driving. I've been up for almost thirty hours straight, with only a few spurts of sleep in between calls. I miss my pillow, and my eyes won't stay open.

"How many have you done so far today?" Dad asks.

"I think seven, but I don't even know what day it is anymore."

"You've done eight. If you stay on and make it ten, I'll give you a bonus."

"If you knew I'd done eight today, why the fuck did you ask me how many?"

"Never mind. Do you want a bonus or not?"

"Depends, I guess. What's the bonus?"

"If you do ten calls in one day, you get a hundred dollars. And that's ten coroner calls, none of those easy calls where you pick up a prepped body and take it to a funeral home."

"Wait, last week I did fourteen in one day and you never said anything about a bonus. When did this start?"

"I started offering the bonus, like, six months ago. Did I forget to tell you about it before now?" he asks, blasé about the whole topic.

"You've *never* mentioned this before right now!"

"Hey, come on. You don't have to yell. Just tell me yes or no if you want some extra cash."

"Fine. If I'm only two away, I'll stay on. But that's it. I'm doing ten and then I'm done. No phone calls, no knocks on my door. You let me sleep for at least twelve hours."

"Okay, okay, fine."

I slam my phone shut and take a deep breath. Six months. Six fucking months he's been offering everyone but me a bonus. Classic Dad power move.

I head to Lucille's with Joel. French Dip sandwiches are on the menu today and I'm drooling just thinking about one. Joel is just coming on shift. Sometimes it happens like that, one exhausted guy from day shift gets paired with a fresh guy on the swing shift around dinner time.

"Has my dad ever offered you a bonus?"

"Ten for a hundred bucks, you mean?"

"What the fuck! Today is literally the first time he's ever mentioned it to me. I've done ten in a day lots of times!"

"Your dad's a cheap fucker. I'm still trying to figure out how I'm going to pay Revenue Canada *and* pay for the wedding. Especially since Myrna wants real doves released after the ceremony."

"That shit's fucked! The doves and the taxes, I mean. I never thought it was weird we didn't get paystubs, but I never thought he was stealing, either!"

"The goddamn doves, that's all she talks about. Your dad swears he paid the taxes."

"Of course he fucking does. He never shows us any proof though, does he?"

"Nope."

My phone vibrates in my pocket. I check, debating whether to jump on answering it. It's my dad, but my sandwich is only half eaten and I don't feel like being interrupted. If it's that important that I can't finish my food, he'll call Joel. A few seconds after my phone stops ringing, Joel's phone blares the most obnoxious sound I've ever heard. For some reason, Joel thinks the best ringtone in the world is the old-timey wail of a siren. Curse the man who made that awful sound a ringtone.

"Hello? Okay. Yep. Got it."

"What is it?"

"Nothing crazy. We have time to finish eating. It sounds like it's going to take a while to get the body out anyway."

"Get it out of where?"

"Some homeless guy was living in the attic of his ex-girlfriend's apartment."

"You got all that from my dad in a thirty second conversation?"

"Yeah, why? How do your calls with him usually go?"

"Not like that. He never gives me any details, just where to go and to hurry up."

"I guess he likes me more." Joel's joking, but I doubt he's far off.

We finish our meals and head out. When we get to the scene, the fire department is hacking a hole in the roof of the apartment building. It's an old Victorian house split into apartments, and all I can think as they hack into the roof is what a damn shame it is to ruin such a cool old house.

It's a strange sight to see, once we have a view through the open roof. It's like finding a mummified mouse that died behind the fridge. The dead man's body is crouched over with one hand on the side of his face, his arm pinned against his body, and the other arm sticking straight up in the air. It might be the exhaustion talking, but he looks like a pharaoh. Mostly because he has a striped sweatshirt tied on his head like the fancy headdress of King Tut. Are we unearthing the tomb of a man who is currently making his way through the underworld, across the river of the damned to reach paradise?

No. This is just a homeless guy who stalked his ex and shot drugs into his toes, and I've been watching way too much of The History Channel.

The position of the dead man and the roof debris make it impossible for me and Joel to make our way into the structure to retrieve the man. The firemen use a cherry picker lift to angle in, and they're kind enough to pull him out for us. It isn't the most graceful retrieval I've ever seen, but at least I didn't have to get in that lift and get him myself. I hate heights. They scare me to my core. Joel and I take the body in an awkward handoff from the firemen in the lift. They dangle his body down to us on the ground. When the lift is completely down, it's still at least seven feet from the ground. Joel grabs the feet and as they lower him and I catch the upper half.

We get him on a stretcher and into the van. One down, one to go before I get to see my bed.

CHAPTER THIRTY

We drop off the body and hang at the morgue with James until the next call comes in. The three of us sit in the morgue office watching weird viral videos on YouTube. Three minutes into another video of a dad getting hit in the balls by his kid, I start to drift into a peaceful sleep, sitting in James' leather chair in the corner of his office. My phone rings and jerks me out of my almost-sleep. This is it, the tenth call. This is the last one before I can go home, eat a few microwave burritos, take a dump, and call it a day. I want nothing more than to climb into bed, turn on an old rerun of *Cops* on TV, and drift off to the Land of Nod. I answer and my dad barks some simple directions at me.

"Get to the intersection of Olive and 77th. MVA, head on, one body."

"Got it. Get your cash ready."

Joel drives because I can't see straight and we make it there in record time. It's well past

1 a.m. and there's almost no one on the road. We find the wreck easily. It looks like a man in a Mazda sped through a stop sign and slammed into a tree on the side of the road.

"Remember, these car accidents can get messy, and if he has a head injury and you jostle him around, you're going to get covered in blood."

"I know, I know. I got this," Joel says.

While I start on the paperwork, I hear Joel mumbling to himself as he tries to wiggle the dead man out of the car.

"You good, or do you need my help?" I shout.

"I'm good." He doesn't sound good. "This guy is just…really big, and wedged between his seat and the dashboard."

"How big?"

"I mean, he's probably only three-fifty or so, but he's tall. I think I've got it, I just need to angle him in the other direction. Why would a guy this size drive a tiny car like this?" Joel trails off and grunts, trying in vain to move the man's dead weight.

I watch in slow motion as Joel jerks the man from side to side. I assume he's trying to free him from where he's wedged, but I also know what's coming before it happens. I watch in horror as on the third jerk a huge slosh of blood spills from the man's cracked-open skull and splashes like a giant wave over Joel's face and upper torso. Joel screams and jumps backward violently, dry heaving and snorting.

"It went up my nose! I got his blood up my nose! Don't say it, don't say 'I told you so'. I know I was supposed to be more careful, but I just wanted to get some leverage on the left side so I could ease him out." Joel frantically tries to clear out his nostrils, which look like they've been thoroughly coated in the dead man's blood. Joel's white shirt is soaked with blood and it's splashed in his hair.

We get the dead guy out of the car with some help from the jaws of life—or as we call them, the jaws of death. I've never seen them used to save anyone. The sheriff on site lends a hand along with the first responders and together we hoist the dead man on the gurney with some serious effort. At least we don't have to be as careful since the entire liquid contents of his head have already been emptied on Joel.

At the hospital we pull around the back, hoping to unload the body straight into the morgue without having to bother with the front door traffic, but tonight they've re-routed all official vehicles to the front door, thanks to a bomb scare called in by a whacko just before we arrive.

Joel circles the hospital and pulls up to the front door where the ambulances normally park. He walks into the harsh lights of the ER waiting room first with the paperwork while I bring in the gurney with the dead guy. It's tough to manage such a large guy by myself, but not impossible. A small woman watching TV in the corner of the waiting room lets out a gut-wrenching scream at the sight of Joel. In the well-lit lobby, he looks like he stepped right out of a horror movie. Immediately, doctors and nurses rush over, worried that Joel's been mortally wounded. There are shouts for a wheelchair and a flurry of hands trying to figure out where he's injured.

After a stunned moment, Joel laughs. With every second that passes of him laughing without explanation, people recoil in fear, unsure of what's happening, until finally he says something.

"This isn't my blood, it's the stiff I'm bringing in. I work with the coroner's office, but the back door is closed off, so they told us to bring him through the front. See, there's my partner." He points to me and the gurney. I wave and smile, trying to break the tension of the moment.

Everyone who flocked to Joel hastily departs to clean the blood off themselves. I can hear the annoyed grumbling.

"Oh man, I wish we had a camera for that. That was so cool! I bet that would have gone viral in no time!" Joel laughs.

CHAPTER THIRTY-ONE

I watch her chest rise and fall in the early morning light for twenty minutes when the thought hits me: someday, she's going to die. At any moment, she could die. What's the point of falling in love with someone who will just end up like all the rest I've seen? Will she be human soup in a bathtub? Maybe her arm will be torn off when she's hit by a train. Or maybe her bloated body will wash up on the north shore.

Tonight was our third date. Paige came to see me and Joel play at The Chop Shop, a shitty dive bar. We drank and watched the rest of the show, then headed downtown for some late-night sushi and ended up back at my place. Her sleeping nakedness seemed so out of place in my bed at first, but watching her snore softly next to me feels completely natural. I'm tired of being lonely. She's full of life, and so genuinely kind and fun to be with that the rest of the world melts away. Like a normal couple that would get up in the morning, drink coffee together, and then head off to work. Except she would no doubt be elbow deep in a cadaver at some point in her day and I would pick up the dead and bring them to her.

She rolls onto her side and faces me. Her calm face is so peaceful, she looks like an angel. A dead angel, thanks to her porcelain skin. My mind flashes an image of her face after rats have eaten her nose.

What the fuck is wrong with me?

Stop. Stop. Stop. Stop. Stop. Stop picturing her dead. Fuck.

I finally get it. I finally understand why most people in this industry are single. It's the fear. If all you see all day long is death, eventually you have to think about the fact that everyone you love will die.

What if they die painfully? What if I'm the one called to pick them up? The only way to cope is to not let anyone get close. You can't think about your girlfriend dying because it's the worst thing you can imagine, so you just shut off those feelings of love and connection. That way when it happens, you're protected from the agony. If you never fall in love, you're just picking up someone you'll miss. You can keep going.

Never let anyone in. Never love anyone. Shut it all down. It makes sense that it's the only way. I can't fall in love with this woman. I won't. It would end me to have something happen to her.

"What's wrong?" Paige asks. "You look like you haven't slept."

I didn't realize she was awake. "I haven't. I can't seem to sleep, even when I have a day off. It's like my body doesn't remember how to sleep anymore. I only slept for about an hour."

"That's going to make you go crazy. You have to get some real REM sleep."

"I know. I try, but it never comes. Even when I take sleeping pills, they only work for a couple hours, then I'm back awake."

"You're so tired, though. You can't possibly be thinking straight." She smiles, her beautiful big eyes crinkling at the corners. I get another flash of her face with the skin rotted and falling off.

Fuck. Fuck. Fuck.

"I'm fine. I don't need a mom. I don't need you to make sure I get enough sleep."

"Okay...sorry. I was just...never mind. I'll get going. I have to be at work in a couple hours. Want to get some food?"

"Nope. I'm good."

She looks at me with her mouth hanging open in shock for a second before she climbs out of my bed and grabs her clothes. "I'll see you later," she says as she hastily pulls on her coat and boots. "I had a good time last night."

"Cool. Later." I know what a huge dick I'm being, but it's better if she doesn't get too attached. Better for both of us.

CHAPTER THIRTY-TWO

The time is finally here. My first Mr. Plow album. All the long days and longer nights, all the bodies and the bullshit…it was all for this. This is my way into the music business. This will help me go on tour. This is my escape from the horrible life that I don't want.

Holding the CD in my hands, I feel all the possibilities of my life open up in front of me. I recorded it over three days in the studio with my producer. Just he and I, working out every tiny detail, every sound, every tone. All of it was mine, and I vibrated with joy the entire time. I finally felt at home, like I was doing exactly what I was born to do. It felt like an eternity waiting to get the final CD, but it was all worth it. This moment was worth everything. Today I'll book my first tour across Canada. Tomorrow I'll walk into the office to quit and tell my dad to fuck off for good.

My phone rings, and when I see who it is my heart races with excitement. "Hey, how's it going?"

"I'm good. What are you doing?" Paige asks. I haven't talked to her since she left my room last week.

"I'm standing on the corner of Main and Charter holding a copy of my first CD, hot off the press. What are you doing?"

"I'm sitting in the King Beef Noodle restaurant across the street, watching you ogle your CD," she laughs.

I jerk my head up and see her waving at me from the front window of the noodle house where she sits alone at a small table.

"Want some company?"

"Sure!"

I head across the street, trying not to skip from pure happiness as I go. As I walk in, she stands and wraps her arms around my neck and plants a kiss on my cheek which makes me blush uncontrollably. Today she smells like marshmallows.

"I've missed you. You never called after I left."

"I know, I'm sorry. I've been busy recording this album. Can you believe it? Look at it!" I shove the CD at her and her face lights up.

"*Parts Unknown*. That's a cool name for it."

"Thanks. How have you been?"

"I've been good, just working. There was a fire in the valley yesterday and a whole family of eight died, so that was a crazy long day," she says, looking down at her noodles.

We sit in silence for a moment. She stirs her soup and I pretend not to notice that she's struggling to figure out how to bring up something uncomfortable.

"So, what happens now? You've got your album done. What's next?"

"Quit my horrible fucking job and go on tour. Make music my career."

"Oh…wow. I won't get to see you every day anymore. That's going to suck."

"Nah, it'll be fine."

She looks straight into my eyes. She looks so sad it hurts my heart a little. "I know what you're doing," she says, sniffling.

"What are you talking about?"

"You're not the first guy in this industry I've dated. I've been through this before."

"Been through what?"

"This. There are two ways this goes but it always ends the same. Either the guy is completely shut down emotionally from the job and there's no point in trying to connect on a deeper level because they just can't, or they compartmentalize everything from the job so much that they disconnect from the rest of the world. I'm guessing you're the first. Either way, it always ends badly."

"Wow, I didn't realize you were a corpse groupie. I'm just one in a long line of corpse draggers, am I?"

Fuck! Why did I say that? The minute it comes out I regret it. I see the hurt on her face.

"No, it's not like that. Why are you being so mean?"

"I'm not, I'm just telling it like it is. Sounds like you have a disgusting fetish for people in the funeral industry!" I'm getting mad and I don't even know why.

"Wow, Dave. I thought you were different. We connected on so many things, I thought we were on the same page."

"Well, you thought wrong I guess."

There's no going back now.

"If you ever grow up and decide to act like an adult instead of a fucking teenager, give me a call. Until then, don't call me."

"You don't have to ask me twice." I stand and slam my chair back.

Fuck! How did this go so badly so quickly? I want to wrap my arms around her and tell her our children would be beautiful and that I want to spend every minute of my life with her. That's never going to happen now that I've treated her like trash.

I stomp out of the restaurant and down the block. Well, fuck it. I was lonely before, I can be lonely again. I'll be fine. Except she's the only person who understands what it's like in this business. I'll call her tomorrow and apologize…maybe. Fuck, I don't know. Damn it. Today was such a good day.

CHAPTER THIRTY-THREE

It's finally here. My last day on the job. I wake up, have breakfast, leave for the office, and immediately notice my eighty-nine-year-old neighbor, Mrs. Frank, wandering from one side of the street to the other, calling for her cat. She does this every single day, despite the fact that her cat has been dead for years.

I pull over and help her out of the street, as I've done many times before. This morning she's wearing what my roommates call her royal cape and crown, AKA a light green housecoat with holes along the bottom hem and a shower cap. Her face is cut with such deep wrinkles it looks like she's frowning despite her joy at seeing me.

"Oh David, thank you. You know, I used to know your grandfather."

"I know, Mrs. Frank. You two were good friends."

"You know, if I had been a braver woman when I was younger, I would have asked your grandfather on a date when I had the chance."

"You would have?"

"Oh, sure! Everyone in the synagogue knew when your grandmother died that there was only a small window of time before one special lady snapped up Sal. He was handsome and rich and...rich," she laughs as I guide her back to her driveway.

"Well, I didn't realize he was such a catch. You have a nice day, Mrs. Frank."

"Thank you dear, you too. And if you see my cat Peanut Butter, you send him home."

"I will, I promise." I head back to the van and glimpse my keys dangling from the ignition on the other side of my securely locked door. Forty-five minutes later I'm finally back on the road, my wallet now fifty dollars lighter. Halfway to the office my phone rings.

"We've got a call I need you to get to," my dad barks sharply.

"I need to talk to you. I was coming to meet you at the office."

"I'm not there. I'm stuck downtown at the police station. I need you to run point on this one."

"What are you doing at the police station?"

He hangs up before I can get another word in. Fuck. A text comes in with just an address. I guess I can do one last call. After this one, I'll be done for good.

The Unicorn Inn and Suites, that's the address. A notoriously sad, drug-riddled motel on the east side of the city. I hate these places. The desk clerks never do room checks like they're supposed to. Every day they're supposed to check on the long-term guests to make sure they're not dead and rotting away inside the room, but the clerks never fucking do it. Why? Because they make six dollars an hour. Because they don't care, and they don't take pride in their job. Because they just don't fucking want to. Either way, it's a huge issue because if they don't make sure that people aren't dead, those people tend to die and rot and make a huge mess that I have to come and deal with. I have to scoop up the chunks of what's left of the person who checked in and promptly OD'd. They sit for who knows how long in the bath, bloating and rotting. If the clerk does the room checks, I just get a normal dead body.

I see the clerk and recognize him instantly.

Jimmy.

I fucking hate Jimmy. Jimmy never does his room checks. Six times in the last year I've come here only to find someone so badly decomposed they can't even be identified because Jimmy doesn't do his goddamn room checks.

Jimmy is in his thirties and has undeserved confidence for a man who's never paid his own bills a day in his life. He wanders around the motel as if he has no place to be. His long stringy hair is often half pulled back into a little greasy ponytail. He always wears button up shirts dotted with stains, and none of his pants have the knees intact. He smells like cigarettes and moth balls.

My rage boils up. One thing. It's one little thing that takes thirty seconds, at most. The one thing that can prevent so much extra work and heartbreak for family members when they have to identify a bloated, nightmarish corpse in hopes of recognizing their loved one. One thing, and he never fucking does it. One thing that matters more than any other thing.

Joel pulls in behind me in the cramped parking lot of the motel. "Hey Dave, you okay? You look pissed."

"You see who's working the front desk today? Jimmy. That fuckwit Jimmy. I have a bad feeling about this one."

"How much you wanna bet he didn't do his room checks this week?"

Joel and I make our way into room six to join the rest of the first responders. What do we find? A puddle. A puddle that used to be a person in the bathtub. A person who shot up, climbed into a nice warm bath, drowned, and then sat in putrid bath water for a week, rotting. I stop dead in my tracks and set the gurney down.

"You okay?" Joel asks.

I turn and head for the door of the motel room. Something in me has finally snapped. I'm fucking done. Jimmy stands smoking outside the motel office. I barrel toward him with one thing in mind: he's going to learn to do his goddamn room checks, if it's the last thing anyone ever teaches him.

His small, rail-thin body shakes with fear the closer I get to him. My face twitches with rage and he backs away from me as fast as he can.

"Jimmy! Don't you dare fucking move!"

"Dave, how's it going man? What's good? Everything okay?"

"Come here!" I shout as he scrambles to back away. His eyes dart back and forth, looking desperately for someone to save him from me, but no one steps forward. I grab Jimmy by the shirt and drag him kicking and shouting across the parking lot to room six.

"What are you doing, Dave? *Dave!* Dave, what are you doing?"

Everyone—cops, first responders, other residents, anyone who sees me coming with him—move out of my way. I drag him over the threshold and into the room, across the orange carpet, past the sad bed with the sunken middle from so many years of overuse. I drag him straight into the bathroom, grab him by the back of the neck, and push his face down toward the bathtub. Jimmy violently wrenches his body away from the tub, eyes closed and screaming. He starts dry heaving.

"You open your eyes, Jimmy! You look and see what happens when you don't do your room checks! You look and see what you leave for other people to deal with when you don't do your fucking job!" I'm shaking and yelling, totally unhinged. He opens his eyes for a moment and then clamps his hands over them, continuing to scream. I let him go and he runs as fast as his little legs can carry him out of the bathroom and into the parking lot, where he pukes his guts out.

Everyone stands around silently watching. I turn to Joel. He grins triumphantly at me.

"Well, he has to learn to do his room checks!" I shout at no one in particular.

CHAPTER THIRTY-FOUR

"I can't believe Myrna talked you into a church wedding."

"I know, I know. But what can I say? She's a sucker for tradition, and I'm a sucker for her," Joel says.

We've been standing at the alter for the past twenty-five minutes, waiting for Myrna to make her entrance. Joel nervously picks at his cuticles the whole time and I'm ready to scream at him to stop. He picks, shoves a finger into his mouth, chews off a chunk of skin, and spits it on the floor behind him. The priest standing next to us clears his throat a couple of times, trying to get Joel's attention, but with no luck. I finally elbow him hard in the ribs.

"Stop eating your fingers already. It's fucking gross."

"I know, I'm sorry. I'm just nervous."

"It's fine. She's probably just fixing her hair or something. She'll be here." I glance down at my black jacket, shiny rental shoes, lilac shirt, and cummerbund the color of pistachio ice cream. Purple and green. Of course Myrna had to choose two hideous colors.

The first notes of "Here Comes the Bride" ring out and we all look toward the back of the church. Myrna stands with her father—who must be a hundred years old—in a white dress that looks like it would be more appropriate for a wedding in the eighteenth century than today. The high collar and long sleeves are the exact opposite of something I would want to see on the woman I'm marrying. I don't see the point in any of this, but whatever makes Joel happy, I'll show up for.

The ceremony is short, and then it's on to the reception at a Moose Lodge a few blocks away. The run-down old Moose Lodge is dark and reeks of cigarette smoke and bleach. It's so dark it takes my eyes a minute to adjust, even though it's only 2 p.m. and outside is sunny and warm.

Someone's hung a banner that says "Congratulations Joel and Myrna" from the rafters in the middle of the room. The tables are each set with paper plates and a giant vase of white carnations.

I make my way to the bar and order two shots and a beer. I don't want to be sober today. I don't want to be reminded how bad I fucked things up with Paige, or how everyone but me seems to be happy and in love and well rested and content with their lives. I can't even imagine how that feels, to wake up every morning not filled with dread and anger.

Everyone from work is here, along with a ton of other people I don't know. I haven't seen Paige yet but I'm sure she'll be here and I don't want to see her.

"And now, it's time for the couple's first dance," the DJ announces over the PA system set up in the corner by the slot machines. The first few notes of "Kiss Me" by Sixpence None the Richer start to play and I can't stop myself from rolling my eyes. I down both shots and chug my beer.

"Two more, and another beer."

"How about just the beer," the bartender says flatly. The look on his lined, weathered face tells me he's not in the mood to overserve me.

"Fine." I light a smoke and sit at the bar with my back to the room so I don't have to look at all the people gazing adoringly at the happy couple.

"What a fucking song, am I right?" James asks as he plops down on the stool next to me.

"Seriously, are we at a fucking high school dance?"

"How's it going, Dave? I haven't seen you since the thing at the motel when you lost your shit. You know you made that guy piss his pants, right?"

"Yeah, I guess I did."

"Oh well. That guy's a fucking tool."

"I don't really want to talk about it."

"Okay... How are you?"

"Fine."

"Okay. Well, I'm going to go hit on Joel's cousin Shirley. She looks like Celine Dion and I think that makes me like her more."

"Good luck. She's got an ugly face. Maybe you can ride her like a donkey. You usually can with ugly chicks, they don't have any self-esteem so they'll do the degrading shit."

"Wow, what the fuck is wrong with you Dave? That's horrible!"

"Tell me I'm wrong after you bang her in the bathroom of this shithouse." The drunker I get, the less I'm able to keep my shitty mood to myself. James walks off in a huff, mumbling to himself.

I hate these people. I hate myself. I hate my job and my dad and this whole rotten goddamn world.

"It's time for the best man's speech!" the DJ announces over the PA.

Shit, that's me. I'm supposed to give my speech. I search my pockets but can't find the paper I wrote it on. I stand and realize how drunk I really am. I can't seem to make my feet walk in a straight line, so I stumble toward the microphone that's held out to me from the DJ stand. I grab it as I bump into the table and knock the DJ's drink onto the floor, smashing the glass.

"Oh shit, sorry! Sorry about that."

I see the look on Joel's face. He does the math. We've been in the building for less than a half hour and I've had two shots and two beers already. His eyes widen and he stares at me, willing me not to fuck this up from the table across the room where he sits with Myrna.

"Joel! And Myrna, of course. You two are...married now." My mind swirls, grasping at something, *anything* to say to this room full of people. "You met and you decided to get married, and that's cool, I guess, if you're into that kind of thing. Myrna has way too many cats and Joel picks up dead people for money, so, you know, that's something..."

Joel frantically pulls his finger across his throat, begging me to stop talking.

"I don't know why anyone would want to get married. Someday the other person is going to die, and you're going to have to find them dead in the tub. Or they'll get hit by a car and you'll hope that all the pieces of their head get filled in with molding clay before the open casket at the funeral..."

James comes at me from out of nowhere, trying to grab the microphone from me, but I manage to dodge him.

"Wait, *wait!* I have one more thing to say! I hope you two are happy, I really do. I love you, Joel. You're the best. I hope you have a long, happy life, and you never have to scrape her corpse out of the bottom of a rotten bathtub."

The whole room groans and murmurs. I feel the stares of the happy people hating me. James grabs me by the arm and drags me off toward the front door.

"Get the fuck off me!" I shout as he pushes me out the door and I stumble into the parking lot.

"Get your shit together, man. Just because you're miserable doesn't mean the rest of the world should be too."

"Fuck off! Why don't you go fuck your donkey-faced bitch!"

James shakes his head at me. The look of pity on his face make me feel nothing but shame.

"Dave, I mean this as your friend. You need a fucking therapist. Something in you is broken. When I first met you, you were funny, and fun, and full of life. Now every time I see you you're mean and grouchy, and half the time you don't make sense when you talk. Seriously, you need some time off." And with that he slams the door shut.

"Fuck you! Don't tell me what I need, motherfucker!" Tears run down my face, but I'm not sad. I'm fucking angry. I need to get away from all these fucking people.

I walk to my van and catch a glimpse of a tall woman in a hot pink dress with her arm around the waist of a skinny blonde guy. It takes a second for me to realize it's Paige. I'm standing drunk in a parking lot with tears running down my face in a purple shirt. Of course this is when she would show up.

"Hi Dave."

"Hey. I was just leaving."

"Okay, well...see ya, I guess."

I wait until the door to the building shuts before I puke all over the side of my van.

CHAPTER THIRTY-FIVE

I roll over in bed and open my eyes. The pain in my head is what stirred me from my drunken sleep. I don't know what time it is, but I know that I'm home. I look down and see I'm still wearing my wedding attire. There's puke on my rental shoes. Not a good sign. I stand to head for the bathroom and on my way I look out the front window of the house. My van is parked on the lawn, the driver's-side door hanging open. Also not a good sign.

In the bathroom I switch on the light and for a second I don't recognize myself. There's blood caked in my hair and a giant gash down my forehead to my cheek. There's leaves and dirt all over my clothes and fur in the cuff of one of my sleeves. Fur?

I get in the shower and wash away all the muck and blood. I remember getting thrown out of Joel's wedding reception, but nothing after that. As I towel off, I get flashes of the day and night before.

Me, driving to McDonald's. Me, eating a fish sandwich in my van in the parking lot. Me, driving down my street, but now it's nighttime.

What happened in between?

Me, swerving to avoid hitting a squirrel. Me, slamming my van into a tree in my neighbor's front yard and smashing my head into my dashboard. Me, parking on my lawn. Me, cuddling with my roommates' cats.

I dress and make some coffee. As I drink it and trying to shake off my hangover, there's pounding on the front door. Not a knock, but a persistent, aggressive pounding. I get up to answer and remember I haven't moved my van yet. There's an undercover cop car in the driveway. Shit. Maybe someone saw me hit the tree and called it in.

I answer the door and on my front porch stands a short man in his late fifties with a thick black mustache and a shiny black pompadour.

"I need to speak with David," he barks at me.

"I'm David."

"I need you to come down to the station with me. I have some questions for you."

"Look, I have insurance. I can give my neighbor my info. You don't have to arrest me over a tree. Besides, I work for the coroner's service. You probably know my dad."

"I don't care what you did to your neighbor's tree, and I'm well aware of who your father is. I'm with homicide."

"Homicide? What the fuck is going on?"

The corners of his mouth curve into a half smile at catching me off guard. "Just get your shoes on and come with me. We'll talk about everything down at the station."

We get to the police station and I recognize some of the faces on duty. The detective leads me to an interview room and has me sit in a hard-plastic chair on one side of an old table. The giant two-way mirror in front of me gives no clues as to who is on the other side. The detective hasn't said a word the entire drive here. Maybe something worse than drunk driving happened last night. I would remember that though, wouldn't I?

"David, I'm Detective Ramirez, and this is Detective Kray," the mustached man says. He points to another short man, this one fat and red faced with the bulbous nose of a drunk.

"What is this about? Why am I here?"

"Do you know a man named Silas Westbrook?"

"No."

The detectives glance at each other and Ramirez shuffles some papers in a beige folder. "Does this help?" he asks, throwing a picture at me. It's of an elderly man in a suit and tie sitting in a pose you would see at a Sears Portrait Center.

"Nope."

"What about this?" Ramirez shoves another picture at me, this one of a rotten corpse in a hole in the dirt. Nothing in the picture gives any clues as to where the hole is located.

"Nope. Can I have a coffee? I'm hungover and I need a smoke."

"Kray, get him a coffee. We're gonna be here awhile. Go ahead and have a smoke." He nods at me.

Kray gets up and shuffles out, slamming the door behind him. He obviously doesn't like being sent on a coffee run.

"What is your father's full name?"

I tell him and he nods his head, as if agreeing with me.

"Do you know if your father has any enemies? Or run-ins with anyone he would have had problems with?"

"My dad is an asshole who doesn't like to pay his taxes or his vendors. He's always fucking people over on business deals and he thinks he'll never get caught. So I guess that makes for a wide array of people who would qualify as enemies."

"Okay, here's the deal. We got a tip that there was a body illegally buried in the back of your father's cemetery. We dug right where the tip told us to and that's where we found the body of Mr. Silas Westbrook. We've sent the body off for an autopsy to figure out the cause of death. But why would your dad, a funeral director, illegally bury a body unless it was because he was worried about the cause of death?"

The door opens and in comes Kray with the tiniest paper cup of coffee I've ever seen.

"I don't know why he would have done that. He doesn't really confide in me, so I have no idea what he does."

Ramirez, annoyed with me, shuffles through his papers again. Watching him shuffle, it dawns on me. The old guy from the parking garage, the one who was in the morgue for a year in a drawer. I never heard what happened to him after he left the morgue. Fuck. This looks bad, that's for sure, but at worst it's an illegal burial, not a murder.

"I think I know what you're talking about," I say.

Ramirez's head shoots up and he nods at me to continue.

"There was this old guy, no family or anything. We picked him up and stored him for a few weeks in the garage because we didn't have a cooler. Then we took him to the morgue and he stayed in a drawer there for over a year. I don't know why. My dad just kept saying he needed to get the paperwork together for his burial. Then one day the morgue called and said they needed the drawer and that we had to get the body out of there. I wasn't the one who got him, so I never thought about where he ended up. I bet that body is this guy."

"Wait, his body was stored in the parking garage?"

"Yeah. It was fucked up. I don't know why he told the man at the old folk's home we could store him. We definitely couldn't. I threw a fit when I found out he was still back there, stinking up the whole place."

"So, let me get this straight. This guy dies of 'natural causes'," Ramirez says, pinching his fingers in air quotes. "The nursing home where he lives calls your dad to come get his body instead of the police, your dad claims to have a fridge to keep him in even though he doesn't, and then you call in a favor to keep him at the morgue for a year?"

"I mean, I didn't call in the favor—it wasn't my job—but yeah, pretty much."

"So how did he get in the hole in the cemetery?"

151

"I don't know. My dad must have had someone dig a grave for him. Wait, who called in the tip? Who told you about the body?"

"It was anonymous."

"Well, I know my dad didn't kill anybody. Especially this guy."

"Just wait here. We'll be right back."

An hour and a half pass before they come back. I just sit there, thinking about everything that's led me to this moment. This is so fucking crazy. I don't belong here. Because of my dad I've been called in by Revenue Canada and now homicide. This is un-fucking-believable.

"Alright, you can go. But don't leave town. If we need more info, you're going to have to come back in."

"Wait, you drove me here. How am I supposed to get home?"

"That lady coroner is here. I bet she could give you a ride."

"Paige? Why is she here?"

"She's the one who autopsied Mr. Westbrook for us."

"I'll pass. Can I use your phone to call a ride?"

CHAPTER THIRTY-SIX

My mom picks me up from the police station and drives me home. As soon as I get there, I grab my keys and my phone and head out the door to find my dad. I need to see him face to face.

I pound on the front door of his house. His wife answers the door.

"He's in the shower. Come back later. He's in a terrible mood."

"Goddamnit, where is that other suitcase?" Dad shouts from upstairs.

I push my way in the door. There are suitcases all over the front room and it looks like someone has ransacked the entire first floor of the house. "Are you going somewhere?" I shout up at him.

My dad comes stomping out of the bedroom, a towel wrapped around his waist. The little bit of hair left on top of his head is still wet from his shower. "What are you doing here?"

"I came to find out why the fuck I was brought in by homicide and spent hours being interrogated."

"Because Reggie is a fucking asshole, that's why!"

"Reggie? The guy who runs the cemetery in the west end of the city?"

"Yes! He's jealous that I'm more successful than him, so he hired some burnout kids that used to dig graves for me and pumped them for information. When he found out I had them bury that old guy with no next of kin, he jumped on the chance to fuck me over. He's going to make sure I lose my license, and he's going to poach all my clients. I'm *ruined!*"

"Technically, you're the one who decided to not do things by the book with the old guy, so it's your own fault."

"Reggie's a goddamn snitch, and he's going to profit off my professional misfortunes!"

"Dad, don't be so dramatic. They won't send you to jail. You didn't kill that guy."

"They won't have the chance to do anything. We're leaving tonight. Sara got a job offer in the states. We're taking your brother and leaving."

"Wait, *what?*"

"Do you want to buy the company? I'll sell it to you for $500,000."

"Dad, you just told me Reggie is going to take all your clients. Even if I had the money to buy it, I wouldn't have any clients left. I'll give you a dollar."

"$495,000."

"One dollar."

"I don't have time for this. Look, I don't know what to tell you. I have to get out before things get worse for me."

"Worse for you? I've been killing myself working this job! And on top of that, the whole thing with Revenue Canada is fucked, too. Us employees are stuck paying back the money you stole!"

"I didn't steal anything. That's a typo on their part."

"A typo?"

"Yes, a typo."

"Then this shit with the police…"

"Look David, I don't know what you want from me. I'm leaving, and I need you to take over the business for me."

"Not in a million fucking years will I take over the business for you."

"Well if you're not going to help me, then leave. I have to pack your brother and we need to leave before they flag my passport."

"I can't believe you're doing this to me… My own father!"

He starts down the stairs, his finger waggling at me as he stomps. "Do you know what my father did to me? He died. That's what he did. He died when I was little. I had to make my way in this world. I was expected to take after him and go into this business, and I made the best of it. You should do the same, instead of crying about how unfair things are for you. You don't know what it means for life to be unfair. You've been handed *everything!* Ingrate!"

We stand nose to nose. His eyes are steely and unflinching.

I pull the office keys and my cell phone out of my pocket and drop them on the floor in front of him.

"So that's it? That's how you're going to handle this? You're not gonna step up and do the right thing?"

"Dad, it's time for me to do the right thing for me," I say calmly.

"You're not a man and you're not my son if you do this!"

"Then I guess I'm neither of those things. I quit."

CHAPTER THIRTY-SEVEN

My dad leaves that night with his wife and my half-brother. He leaves everyone to clean up his mess. He loses his funeral director's license and his business is bought out. On the surface, everything goes back to normal fairly quickly. Joel stays on with the new owner but ends up quitting after a month.

It takes me eight weeks to call Paige. Eight weeks to catch up on sleep. Eight weeks to get back to something that resembles normal, physically and mentally. Eight weeks to swallow my pride.

"Hello?"

"Hey, Paige. It's Dave."

"Hey. I didn't recognize this number."

"Yeah, I had to get a new phone after I quit my job."

"I heard you'd quit. I also heard your dad bailed and fled the country."

"Yep, he did."

"Hmm."

A horrible silence. I can hear her breathing and I close my eyes. I picture her chest rising and falling. Her long curly hair falling on her shoulders. Her smile.

"Listen Paige, I owe you an apology. I don't know when it happened, but I sort of lost my mind for a while there."

Silence.

"And I know I don't deserve a second chance. I was a real asshole. I don't know, maybe you're even dating someone else now, but the truth is, I think about you all the time. I wonder what you're eating for lunch and what show you watch before you fall asleep at night. I wonder if you ever wonder what I'm doing. And mostly I wonder if we can start over and try again now that I'm not, you know...an asshole."

"No."

"No to all of it?"

"I mean no, I'm not dating anyone."

I exhale with relief. "How about this, Paige. Would you like to have dinner with me and see a horror movie double feature at the Victorian Theatre?"

"That sounds like fun."

"It will be. I promise."

CHAPTER THIRTY-EIGHT

The music blares loudly from the speakers in my van. I'm riding a rush of adrenaline as I hit the road on my very first tour as Mr. Plow. I booked an ambitious tour that takes me from the west coast all the way to the east and ends at The Kathedral in Toronto.

I have six boxes filled with fresh-off-the-press copies of my first album and four boxes of T-shirts in various sizes screen printed with my name and a design that Joel drew for me. I have two boxes filled with women's underwear with "Plow Me" screen printed on the front, and a box full of vinyl stickers. The money from my merch will help pay for gas while I'm on the road. I also have a giant map book, a catalog with all the Motel 6 locations across Canada, a carton of smokes, a credit card, a duffle bag with clothes, and a spiral notebook so I can keep all the contact info I get from networking with other bands and bookers. I'm ready.

The wind whips me in the face as I drive down the highway and it feels like the universe pushing me on to the next chapter in my life. I'm intoxicated with the freedom of it all.

I glance down at the picture of Paige by my speedometer. She gave it to me so when I miss her I can still see her perfect, smiling face. I didn't know life could feel like this. I didn't know this force propelling me toward my destiny could feel this good.

I stop for a burger along the way and enjoy sitting by myself at the greasy restaurant, looking out the window. The night terrors are still there.

Every night I wake at least three times, dreaming of rotting corpses dragging me down to hell with them. Sometimes they kiss me on the mouth and suck my soul from between my lips. Sometimes it's my friends and family. Sometimes it's even Paige.

I know that someday we will all die. That hasn't changed. But now I know I won't be the one to pick up the dead when we do. I try to live in the moment and enjoy my life instead of waiting for my death. No more wondering how or when it will come, and how my body will look when they come to take me to the morgue.

I drive on toward the first show. The venue is a small bar in a small town off the highway about three more hours east. As I drive, I see a dead deer on the side of the road, broken and fresh and bleeding. My heart leaps into my throat and panic washes over me.

I remember what the doctor told me to do when this happens: take a deep breath in and count to four, then breathe out for four counts. Then again. And again.

I'm okay. I'm okay. I don't have to deal with that dead body. All I have to do is keep on driving.

Slowly, the panic releases its grip on my throat.

I hate that this happens. I hate that I can be having a normal day and out of nowhere something reminds me of the dead bodies, then I'm right back there, in that job. But it will get better. The more time passes, the further I get from that life.

I arrive at the bar early. It's only 5 p.m. and the show starts in four hours, but that's okay. I can explore the small town. I can sit and make friends with the bartender. I can do anything.

I'm free.

Acknowledgements

Thank you to the best editors, Terri Nicolet and Terry Armstrong, without whom this story would have been much shorter and made much less sense. Thank you Joe Bodner for your memories. Thank you boys for going to bed early so your parents could write this book.

About the Authors

Dave Plow was at one time a body removal technician at his family's business in the death industry. He is a Canadian musician and comedian who has released thirteen albums as Mr. Plow and has played in numerous punk rock and rock bands. Dave has toured and played music for over twenty-five years all over North America.

Erin Potter-Plow is an American writer with a small cult following on her blog. She has written children's books, supernatural thrillers, and short films. Erin has won awards for her short films and performed in Mortified.

Dave and Erin are married and live in Portland, Oregon with their two kids.

Visit the Mr. Plow Facebook page:
https://www.facebook.com/MrPlowTheSoloAcousticAct/

Visit Erin's blog: http://unicorncupcakebrigad.blogspot.com/